Deconstruction III

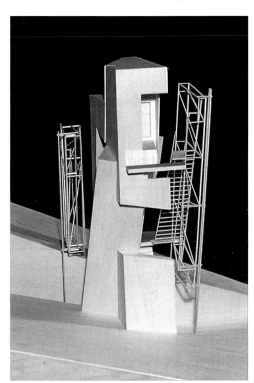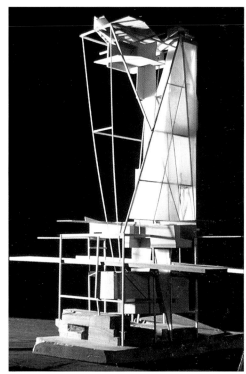

COLUMBIA UNIVERSITY SCHOOL OF ARCHITECTURE: *L TO R*: MICHAEL KENNEDY, TOWER/HOUSE/OBSERVATORY; LAURA BRIGGS, VERTICAL TERMINAL

BERNARD TSCHUMI, ZKM KARLSRUHE

Architectural Design
Edited by Andreas C Papadakis

Deconstruction III

COOP HIMMELBLAU, THE OPEN HOUSE

ACADEMY EDITIONS • LONDON

Editorial Note

With the third issue on the theme in almost as many years, Deconstruction is proving its success as a major direction in architecture today. Once regarded by some as an intellectual process with no immediate bearing on built architecture, architects are now working with Deconstructive theory as an integral part of their practical work. Since the *Architectural Design* Deconstruction II issue, Peter Eisenman's Wexner Center and his Koizumi Lighting Theatre in Tokyo have been realised: two prime examples of the relationship between criticism and construct, theory and practice. Meanwhile, Zaha Hadid's major commission to date displays an exuberance that is realised at the meeting point between theory and the physical, built work. Exuberance is also a befitting description of Frank Gehry's architecture, now commissioned in Europe. Competitions have played a major role in the encouragement of Deconstructionist work, as seen in the Osaka and Groningen pavilions which brought together a number of theoretically orientated architects. The opening essay by Mark Wigley, who has been instrumental in the synthesis of critical theory and the architectural realities, assesses the development of Deconstruction as a thought process and comments on its future. Bernard Tschumi's work continues to remain prominent in the field of Deconstruction. As Dean of the Columbia School of Architecture, his contribution to and influence on the graduate student work cannot be over-estimated: the work shows a desire to both vigorously explore and criticise. *VC*

Acknowledgements

We are grateful to Bernard Tschumi for supplying material for the feature on the student work. The *Architectural Design* Interview with Daniel Libeskind was conducted by Vivian Constantinopoulos. Material for Frank Gehry's design provided by Vitra Ltd. The article by Wolf Prix is an edited version of a lecture given at the RIBA.

Editor
Dr Andreas C Papadakis

EDITORIAL OFFICES: 42 LEINSTER GARDENS, LONDON W2 3AN TELEPHONE: 071 402 2141
CONSULTANTS: Catherine Cooke, Dennis Crompton, Terry Farrell, Kenneth Frampton, Charles Jencks
Heinrich Klotz, Leon Krier, Robert Maxwell, Demetri Porphyrios, Colin Rowe, Derek Walker
HOUSE EDITOR: Maggie Toy DESIGNED BY: Andrea Bettella, Mario Bettella SUBSCRIPTIONS MANAGER: Mira Joka
Staff contributing to this issue: Vivian Constantinopoulos, Kim Russell, Ian Huebner

First published in Great Britain in 1990
New edition published in Great Britain in 1995 by *Architectural Design*
an imprint of
ACADEMY GROUP LTD, 42 LEINSTER GARDENS, LONDON W2 3AN
MEMBER OF THE VCH PUBLISHING GROUP
ISBN: 1 85490 253 9

Architectural Design Profile 87 is published as part of *Architectural Design* Vol 60 9-10/1990

Distributed in the United States of America by
ST MARTIN'S PRESS, 175 FIFTH AVENUE, NEW YORK 10010
ISBN: 1 85490 253 9

Printed and bound in Singapore

MARIE-THERES DEUTSCH, PERMANENT SCULPTURE AT THE FRANKFURT BALLET

Contents

Architectural Design Profile No. 87
Deconstruction III

MARK WIGLEY

THE TRANSLATION OF ARCHITECTURE: THE PRODUCT OF BABEL

How then to translate deconstruction in architectural discourse? Perhaps it is too late to ask this preliminary question. What is left to translate? Or, more important, what is always left by translation? Not just left behind but left specifically for architecture. What remains of deconstruction for architecture? What are the remains that can be located only in architecture, the last resting place of deconstruction? The question of translation is, after all, a question of survival. Can deconstruction survive architecture?

It is now over 20 years since Derrida's first books were published. Suddenly his work has started to surface in architectural discourse. This appears to be the last discourse to invoke the name of Derrida. Its reading seems the most distant from the original texts, the final addition to a colossal tower of readings. It is an addition that marks in some way the beginning of the end of deconstruction, its limit if not its closure.

After such a long delay – a hesitation whose strategic necessity must be examined – there is such a haste to read Derrida in architecture. But it is a reading that seems at once obvious and suspect. Suspect in its very obviousness. Deconstruction is understood to be unproblematically architectural. There seems to be no translation, just a metaphoric transfer, a straightforward application of theory from outside architecture to the practical domain of the architectural object. The hesitation does not seem to have been produced by some kind of internal resistance on the part of that object. On the contrary, there is no evidence of work, no task for the translator, no translation. There is just a literal application, a transliteration. Architecture is understood as a representation of deconstruction, the material representation of an abstract idea. The reception of Derrida's work seems to follow the classical teleology from idea to material form, from initial theory to final practice, from presence to representation. Architecture, the most material of the discourses, seems the most detached from the original work, the most suspect of the applications, the last application, the representational ornament that cannot influence the tradition to which it is added, a veneer masking as much as it reveals of the structure beneath. The last layer, just an addition, no translation. Yet.

But how to translate? Deconstruction is no more than a subversion of the architectural logic of addition which sets in play a certain thought of translation. One cannot simply consider translation outside and above either deconstruction or architecture. The question immediately becomes complicated. There is no hygienic starting point, no superior logic to apply. There are no principles to be found in some domain that governs both deconstructive discourse and architectural discourse. Nevertheless, certain exchanges are already occurring between them. Architecture, translation and deconstruction are already bound together, already defining an economy whose pathological symptoms can be studied. It is a matter of identifying the logic of translation that is already in operation. Since there is no safe place to begin, one can only enter the economy and trace its convoluted geometry in order to describe this scene of translation.

This can be done by locating that moment in each discourse where the other is made thematic, where the other comes to the surface. The line of argument that surfaces there can then be folded back on the rest of the discourse to locate other layers of relationships. These hidden layers are not simply below the surface. They are within the surface itself, knotted together to form the surface. To locate them involves slippage along fault-lines rather than excavation. As there are no principles above or below the convoluted folds of this surface, it is a matter of following some circular line of inquiry, of circulating within the economy, within the surface itself.

Translation surfaces in deconstructive discourse when Derrida, following Walter Benjamin's The Task of the Translator, argues that translation is not the transference, reproduction, or image of an original. The original only survives in translation. The translation constitutes the original to which it is added. The original calls for a translation which establishes a nostalgia for the innocence and the life it never had. To answer the call, the translation abuses the original, transforming it.

> And for the notion of translation, we would have to substitute a notion of transformation: a regulated transformation of one language by another, of one text by another. We never will have, and in fact never have had, a 'transport' of pure signifieds from one language to another, or within one and the same language, that the signifying instrument would leave virgin and untouched.[1]

There is some kind of gap in the original which the translation is called in to cover over. The original is not some organic whole, a unity. It is already corrupted, already fissured. The translation is not simply a departure from the original, as the original is already exiled from itself. Language is necessarily impure. Always divided, it remains foreign to itself. It is the translation that produces the myth of purity and, in so doing, subordinates itself as impure. In constructing the original as original, the translation constructs itself as secondary, exiled. The supplementary translation which appears as a violation of the purity of the work is actually the possibility of that very purity. Its violence to the original is a violent fidelity, a violence called for by the original precisely to construct itself as pure. The abuse of the text is called for by an abuse already within the text. Translation exploits the conflict within the original to present the original as unified.

Consequently, in translation, the text neither lives nor dies; it neither has its original life-giving intention revived (presentation) nor is it substituted by a dead sign (representation). Rather, it just lives on; it survives. This survival is organised by a contract which ensures that translation is neither completed nor completely frustrated.[2] The contract is the necessarily unfulfilled promise of translation. It defines a scene of incomplete translation, an incompletion that binds the languages of the original and translation together in a strange knot, a double bind. This constitutional bond is neither a social contract nor a transcendental contract above both languages. Neither cultural nor 'acultural', it is other than cultural without being outside culture. The negotiable social contracts within which language operates presuppose this non-negotiable contract which makes language possible, establishing the difference between languages while making certain exchanges between them possible.

This translation contract is not independent of the languages whose economy it organises. It is inscribed within both languages. Not only is the original already corrupt, already divided, but translation is occurring across those divisions. The gap between languages passes through each language. Because language is always already divided, inhabited by the other, and constantly negotiating with it, translation is possible.[3] The translation within a language makes possible translation outside it. One language, therefore is not simply outside the other. Translation occurs across a gap folded within, rather than between, each language. It is precisely these folds that constitute language. The contract is no more than the geometry of these folds, the organisation of the gaps.

Consequently, any translation between architecture and deconstruction does not occur between the texts of architectural discourses and those of philosophical discourse.[4] Rather, it occupies and organises both discourses. Within each there is an architectural translation of philosophy as a philosophical translation of architecture. To translate deconstruction in architectural discourse is not, therefore, to recover faithfully some original, undivided sense of deconstruction.[5] Rather, it is one of the abuses of the texts signed by Derrida that constitutes them as originals. To translate deconstruction in architectural discourse is to examine the gaps in deconstructive writing that demand an architectural translation in order to constitute those texts as deconstructive. The architectural translation of deconstruction is literally the production of deconstruction. This production must be organised by the terms of a contract between architecture and philosophy which is inscribed within the structure of both in a way that defines a unique scene of translation.

A preliminary sketch of this scene can be drawn by developing Heidegger's account of the relationship between architecture and philosophy. Heidegger examines the way in which philosophy describes itself as architecture. Kant in his Critique of Pure Reason, for example, describes metaphysics as an 'edifice' erected on secure foundations laid on the most stable ground. Kant criticises previous philosophers for their tendency to 'complete its speculative structures as speedily as may be, and only afterwards to enquire whether these foundations are reliable.'[6] The edifice of metaphysics has fallen apart and is 'in ruins' because it has been erected on 'groundless assertions' unquestioningly inherited from the philosophical tradition. To restore a secure foundation, the critique starts the 'thorough preparation of the ground.'[7] With the 'clearing, as it were, and levelling of what has hitherto been wasteground.'[8] The edifice of metaphysics is understood as a grounded structure.

Heidegger argues that Kant's attempt to lay the foundations is the necessary task of all metaphysics. The question of metaphysics has always been that of the ground (grund) on which things stand even though it has been explicitly formulated in these terms only in the modern period inaugurated by Descartes. Metaphysics is no more than the attempt to locate the ground. Its history is that of a succession of different names (logos, ratio, arche . . . etc) for the ground. Each of them designates 'Being,' which is understood as presence. Metaphysics is the identification of the ground as 'supporting presence' for an edifice. It searches for 'that upon which everything rests, what is always there for every being as its support.'[9] For Heidegger, metaphysics is no more than the determination of ground-as-support.

Metaphysics is the question of what the ground will withstand, of what can stand on the ground. The motif of the edifice, the grounded structure, is that of standing up. Philosophy is the construction of propositions that stand up. The ability of its constructs to stand is determined by the condition of the ground, its supporting presence. Heidegger repeatedly identified presence with standing. The 'fundamental' question of metaphysics (why there are beings rather than nothing) asks of a being 'on what does it stand?'[10] Standing up through construction makes visible the condition of the ground.

However, in Heidegger's reading, construction does not simply make visible a ground that precedes it. The kind of ground clearing Kant attempts does not simply precede the construction of the edifice. The ground is not simply independent of the edifice. The edifice is not simply added to the ground, it is not simply an addition. For Heidegger, a building does not stand on a ground that preceded it and on which it depends. Rather, it is the erection of the building that establishes the fundamental condition of the ground. Its structure makes the ground possible.[11] The ground is constituted rather than revealed by that which appears to be added to it. To locate the ground is necessarily to construct an edifice.

Consequently, philosophy's successive relayings of the foundation do not preserve a single, defined edifice.[12] Rather, it is a matter of abandoning the traditional structure by removing its foundation.[13] The form of the edifice changes as the ground changes. Having cleared the ground, Kant must reassess its load-bearing capacity and 'lay down the complete architectonic plan' of a new philosophy in order to 'build upon this foundation'[14] The edifice must be redesigned. Relaying the foundations establishes the possibility of a different edifice. For Heidegger, the laying of the foundation is the 'projection of the intrinsic possibility of metaphysics'[15] through an interrogation of the condition of the ground. This interrogation is the projection of a plan, the tracing of an outline, the drawing, the designing of an edifice, the drawing of the design out of the ground. Interrogating the condition of the ground defines certain architectonic limits, certain structural constraints within which the philosopher must work as a designer. The philosopher is an architect, endlessly attempting to produce a grounded structure.

In these terms, the history of philosophy is that of a series of substitutions for structure. Every reference to structure is a reference to an edifice erected on a ground, an edifice from which the ground cannot simply be removed. The motif of the edifice is that of a structure whose free play is constrained by the ground. The play of representations is limited, controlled, by presence: 'The concept of centred structure is in fact the concept of a play based on a fundamental ground, a play constituted on the basic of a fundamental immobility and a reassuring certitude, which itself is beyond the reach of play.'[16] Philosophy is the attempt to restrain the free play of representation by establishing the architectonic limits provided by the ground. It searches for the most stable ground in order to exercise the greatest control over representation.

The metaphor of grounded structure designates the fundamental project of metaphysics to identify a universal language which controls representation in the name of presence, a logos. Derrida traces the way that metaphysics maintains its logocentric protocol of presence/presentation/representation with an account of language which privileges speech over writing. While speech is promoted as presentation of pure thought, writing is subordinated as representation of speech. The role of architecture in this hierarchy can be identified by recalling Heidegger's identification of the original sense of the word logos as 'gathering' in a way that lets things stand, the standing of construction. A link between structure and presence organises traditional accounts of language. The means by which language is grounded is always identified with structure. Speech is identified with structure which makes visible the condition of the ground it is bonded to. Phonetic writing, as the representation of speech, is identified with ornament which represents the structure it is added to. If writing ceases to be phonetic, if it loses its bond with speech, it becomes representation detached from pure presence, like an ornament that refers away from the structure it is attached to. The protocol of metaphysics, sustained by the account of language as thought/speech/phonetic writing/nonphonetic writing, is established by the architectural motif of ground/structure/ornament.

Metaphysics is dependent on an architectural logic of support. Architecture is the figure of the addition, the structural layer, one element supported by another. Metaphysics' determination of the ground-as-support presupposes a vertical hierarchy from ground through structure to ornament. The idea of support, of structure, is dependent on a certain view of architecture which defines a range of relationships from fundamental (foundational) to supplementary (ornamental). With each additional layer, the bond is weaker. The structure is bonded to the ground more securely than the ornament is bonded to the structure. But as the distance from the ground becomes greater, the threat to the overall structure diminishes. The vertical hierarchy is a mechanic of control which makes available the thought of the ground-as-support which is metaphysics.

Structure makes present the ground. Structure is grounding, submitting to the authority of presence. Ornament either represents the grounding of structure or deviates from the line of support, detaching itself from the ground in order to represent that which is other than the structure. Philosophy attempts to tame ornament in the name of the ground, to control representation in the name of presence. The philosophical economy turns on the status of ornament. It is the structure/ornament relationship that enables us to think of support, and thereby, to think of the ground.

The strategic importance of this architectural metaphor emerges when Heidegger examines the status of art. Metaphysics's determination of ground-as-support also determines art as merely a representative 'addition' to a utilitarian object, a 'superstructure' added to the 'substructure' which, in turn, is added to the ground. The architectural metaphor organises this relationship: 'It seems almost as though the thingly element in the art work is like the substructure into and upon which the other, authentic element is built.'[17] The material object is the 'support' to which the artwork is added, the presentation of the ground to which the artwork is added as a representation.

But it is not just the internal structure of the art object that is understood in these architectural terms, it is also the status of art as a discourse. Heidegger notes that metaphysics treats art itself as a superstructure added to the substructure of philosophy. Metaphysics understands itself as a grounded structure to which is attached the representational ornament of art. It subordinates the arts, and therefore architecture, by employing the vertical hierarchy dependent on a certain understanding of architecture. Art is subordinated by being located furthest from the ground. Architecture, then, plays a curious strategic role. It is able to pass between philosophy and art in a unique way. It is involved in a kind of translation. The metaphor circulates between and within the two systems, complicating them as it folds back on itself. A convoluted economy is sustained by the description of architecture as ornamented structure, which enables art to be subordinated to philosophy even while philosophy describes itself as architecture. Philosophy describes itself in terms of the very thing which it subordinates.

Heidegger argues that art is actually 'foundational' to the philosophical tradition that subordinates it to the level of ornament. This convolution is doubled in the case of architecture itself. Metaphysics organises itself around an account of the object as grounded structure. It projects an account of architecture outside itself which it then appeals to as an outside authority. It literally produces an architecture. As Derrida argues, in reading the architectural metaphor in Kant's aesthetics, 'Philosophy, which in this book has to think art through – art in general and fine art – as a part of its field or of its edifice, is here representing itself as part of its part, philosophy as an art of architecture. It re-presents itself, it detaches itself, detaches from itself a proxy, a part of itself beside itself in order to think the whole, to saturate or heal over the whole that suffers from detachment.'[18] It does so to cover up some kind of gap, some internal division. Metaphysics produces the architectural object as the paradigm of ground-as-support in order to veil its own lack of support, its ungrounded condition. Philosophy represents itself as architecture, it translates itself as architecture, producing itself in the translation. The limits of philosophy are established by the metaphorical status of architecture.

Philosophy draws an edifice, rather than draws on an edifice. It produces an architecture of grounded structure which it then uses for support, leaning on it, resting within it. The edifice is constructed to make theory possible, then subordinated as a metaphor in order to defer to some higher, non-material truth. Architecture is constructed as a material reality in order to liberate some higher domain. As material, it is but metaphor. The most material condition is used to establish the most ideal order which is then bound to reject it as merely material. The status of material oscillates. The metaphor of the ground, the bedrock, the case, the fundamental, inverts to become base in the sense of degraded, material, less than ideal. The vertical hierarchy inverts itself. In this inversion, architecture flips from privileged origin to gratuitous supplement, foundation to ornament.

Philosophy treats its architectural motif as but a metaphor that can and should be discarded as superfluous. The figure of the grounded structure is but an illustration, a useful metaphor that illustrates the nature of metaphysics but outlives is usefulness and might be abandoned from the final form of metaphysics, a representation to be separated from the fundamental presentation, a kind of scaffolding to be discarded when the project is complete, a frame that traces the outline of the building, a trace that lacks substance but is structurally necessary, an open frame that is the possibility of a closed structure to which it then becomes an unnecessary appendage. Scaffolding is that piece of structure which becomes ornamental. When philosophy reflects upon its own completion, it defines architecture as metaphorical. Metaphysics is the determination of architecture as metaphor.

But can architecture be so simply discarded? The use of the figure of structure 'is only metaphorical, it will be said. Certainly. But metaphor is never innocent. It orients research and fixed results. When the spatial model is hit upon, when it functions, critical reflection rests within it.'[19] The very attempt to abandon metaphors involves metaphors. Even the concept that the metaphorical can be detached from the fundamental is itself metaphorical. Metaphysics grounds itself in the metaphors it claims to have abandoned. Metaphor 'is the essential weight which anchors discourse in metaphysics'[20] rather than a superfluous ornament. Metaphor is fundamental. The metaphor of the grounded structure in particular cannot be discarded in order to reveal the ground itself. The 'fundamental' is itself an architectural metaphor, so architecture cannot be abandoned in favour of the fundamental.

Thus, the criteria for a classification of philosophical metaphors are borrowed from a derivative philosophical discourse . . . They are metaphorical, registering every meta-metaphorics, the values of concept, foundation, and theory . . . What is fundamental corresponds to the desire for a firm and ultimate ground, a terrain to build on, the earth as the support for an artificial structure.[21]

Philosophy can only define a part of itself as non-metaphorical by employing the architectural metaphor. This metaphor organises the status of metaphor. In so doing, it organises the tradition of philosophy that claims to be able to discard it. Architectural figures cannot be detached from philosophical discourse. The architectural metaphor is not simply one metaphor among others. More than the metaphor of foundation, it is the foundational metaphor. It is therefore not simply a metaphor.

The architectural motif is bound to philosophy. The bond is contractual – not in the sense of an agreement signed by two parties, but a logical knot of which the two parties are but a side effect. More than the terms of exchange within and between these discourses it produces each discourse as a discourse. The translation contract between architecture and philosophy works both ways. Each constructs the other as an origin from which they are detached. Each identifies the other as other. The other is constructed as a privileged origin which must then be discarded. In each there is this moment of inversion.

This primal contract, which is neither a contingent, cultural artifact nor an 'atemporal', 'acultural' principle, establishes the possibility of a social contract that separates architecture and philosophy and constitutes them as discourses. The eventual status of architecture as a discipline began to be negotiated by the first texts of architectural theory, which drew on the Canons of the philosophical tradition to identify the proper concern of the newly constituted figure of the architect with drawing (*disegno*) that mediates between the idea and the building, the formal and the material, the soul and the body, the theoretical and the practical. Architecture – architectural drawing – is neither simply a mechanical art bound to the bodily realm of utility, nor a liberal art operating in the realm of ideal, but is their reconciliation, the bridge between the two. Architectural theory, thus, constructs architecture as a bridge between the dominant oppositions of metaphysics and constitutes itself by exploiting the contractural possibility already written into the philosophical tradition wherein it describes itself as architecture.

It is not simply that architecture has some familiar, unambiguous, material reality that is drawn upon by philosophy. Rather, philosophy draws an architecture, presents a certain understanding, a theory, of architecture. The terms of the contract are the prohibition, a different description of the architectural object, or rather, the dissimulation of the object. To describe the privileged role of architecture in philosophy is not to identify architecture as the origin from which philosophy derives, but rather to show that the condition effected when philosophy infects itself from outside, by drawing on architecture, is internal to architecture itself. Architecture is cut from within, and philosophy unwittingly appeals to architecture precisely for this internal torment.

The concern here is to locate certain discursive practices repressed within the pathological mechanisms of this economy, to trace the impact of another account of architecture hidden within the tradition. Deconstruction is not outside the tradition. It achieves its force precisely by inhabiting the tradition, and thereby operating in terms of the contract. The question is, what relationship does deconstruction assume with the account of architecture repressed by the tradition? The translation of deconstruction in architecture does not simply occur across the philosophy/architecture divide. It is occurring within such discourse. It is not a matter of simply generating a new description of the architectural object in architectural discourse but

rather of locating the account of architecture already operates within deconstructive writing. It is the difference between this account and that of traditional philosophy that marks the precise nature of deconstruction's inhabitation of philosophy. The limits of deconstruction are established by the account of architecture it unwittingly produces.

As architecture is bound up into language[22], this account can be located precisely in the discussion of translation itself. In as much as deconstruction tampers with the philosophical ideal of translation, it tampers with the philosophical ideal of architecture.

Derrida's account of translation is organised around an architectural figure: the Tower of Babel. The failure of the tower marks the necessity for translation, the multiplicity of languages, the free play of representation, which is to say the necessity for controlling representation. The collapse marks the necessity for a certain construction. The figure of the tower acts as the strategic intersection of philosophy, architecture, deconstruction and translation.

The tower is the figure of philosophy because the dream of philosophy is that of translatability.[23] Philosophy is the ideal of translation. But the univocal language of the builders of the tower is not the language of philosophy, it is an imposed order, a violent imposition of a single language.[24] The necessity of philosophy is defined in the collapse rather than in the project itself. As the desire for translation produced by the incompletion of the tower is never completely frustrated, the edifice is never simply demolished. The building project of philosophy continues but its completion is forever deferred.

The tower is also the figure of deconstruction. Since deconstruction inhabits philosophy, subverting it from within, it also inhabits the figure of the tower. It is lodged in the tower, transforming the representation of its construction. In as much as philosophy is the ideal of translation, deconstruction is the subversion of translation.[25] That subversion is found within the conditions for philosophy, the incompletion of the tower: 'The deconstruction of the Tower of Babel, moreover, gives a good idea of what deconstruction is: an unfinished edifice whose half completed structures are visible, letting one guess at the scaffolding behind them.'[26] Deconstruction identifies the inability of philosophy to establish the stable ground, the deferral of the origin which prevents the completion of the edifice by locating the untranslatable, that which lies between the original and the translation.

But the tower is also the figure of architecture. The necessity of translation is the failure of building that demands a supplementation by architecture. Just as it is the precondition for philosophy, understood as building (presentation), translation also marks the necessity for architecture (representation), but as a representation that speaks of the essence of building, an architecture that represents the ground in its absence: 'If the tower had been completed there would be no architecture. Only the incompletion of the tower makes it possible for architecture as well as the multitude of languages to have a history.'[27] The possibility of architecture is bound up with the forever incomplete project of philosophy. Philosophy requires the account of building as grounded and architecture as detached precisely because of the incompletion. Structural failure produces the need for a supplement, the need for a building/architecture distinction, the need for architecture. Architecture is the translation of building that represents building to itself as complete, secure, undivided.

Since the tower is the figure of deconstruction, architecture and translation, the question shifts from identifying the common ground between them, the identity, to locating the difference. The once discrete domains become entangled to the extent that the task becomes to identify the convoluted mechanism of translation that produces the sense of separate identities. This mechanism must be embedded in the scene of translation which bears on the status of structure.

Translation between the discourses is made possible by a breakdown in the sense of structure that is the currency within them. Derrida argues that the incompletion of the tower is the very structure of the tower. The tower is deconstructed by establishing that 'the structure of the original is marked by the requirement to be translated'[28] and that it 'in no way suffers from not being satisfied, at least it does not suffer in so far as it is the very structure of the work.'[29] There is a gap in the structure that cannot be filled, a gap that can only be covered over. The tower is always already marked by a flaw in as much as it is a tower. This is a displacement of the traditional idea of structure. Structure is no longer simply grounding. It is no longer a vertical hierarchy but a convoluted line. The structure is no longer simply standing on the ground. The building stands on an abyss.

This argument follows Heidegger's attempt to dismantle the edifice of metaphysics in order to reveal the condition of the ground on which it stood. In doing so, he raises the possibility that the ground (grund) might actually be a concealed 'abyss' (abgrund) such that metaphysics is constructed in ignorance of the instability of the terrain on which it is erected: 'we move over this ground as over a flimsily covered abyss.'[30] Metaphysics becomes the veiling of the ground rather than the interrogation of it.

Heidegger's later work developed this possibility into a principle. He argues that philosophy has been in a state of 'groundlessness' ever since the translation of the ancient Greek terms into the language of metaphysics. This translation substituted the original sense of ground with that of the sense of ground-as-support, ground as supporting presence to which the world is added. For Heidegger, metaphysics is groundless precisely because it determines the ground as support. The original sense of logos has been lost. With metaphysics, the origin is seen as a stable ground rather than as an abyss. The 'modern' crisis, the 'groundlessness' of the age of technology, is produced by philosophy's ancient determination of the ground as support for a structure to which representations are added.[32] The crisis of representation is produced by the very attempt to remove representations in order to reveal the supporting presence of the ground. Man is alienated from the ground precisely by thinking of it as secure.

Because of the very familiarity of the principle of ground-as-support, 'we misjudge most readily and persistently the deceitful form of its violence.'[33] Metaphysics conceals this violence. The architectural motif of the grounded structure is articulated in a way that effects this concealment. The vertical hierarchy is a mechanism of control that veils its own violence.

Heidegger attempts to subvert this mechanism by rereading the status of the architectural motif. He argues that the thought of architecture as a simple addition to building actually makes possible the thought of the naked ground as support. Undermining the division between building and architecture displaces the traditional sense of the ground: 'But the nature of the erecting of buildings cannot be understood adequately in terms either of architecture or of engineering construction, nor in terms of a mere combination of the two.'[34] The thought of that which is neither building nor architecture makes possible the original ground that precedes the ground-as-support. The linear logic of addition is confused. The building is not simply added to the ground, the ornament is not simply added to the structure, art is not simply added to philosophy. The vertical hierar-chy of ground/structure/ornament is convoluted. The architectural motif undermines itself.

But while certain Heideggerian moves subvert the logic of addition by displacing the traditional account of architecture, Heidegger ultimately contradicts that possibility, confirming the traditional logic by looking for a stable structure. Derrida argues that Heidegger is unable to abandon the tradition of ground-as-support. Indeed, he retains it in the very account of translation he uses to identify its emergence.

> At the very moment when Heidegger is denouncing translation into Latin Words, at the moment when, at any rate, he declares Greek speech to be lost, he also makes use of a 'metaphor.' Of at least one metaphor, that of the foundation and the ground. The ground of the Greek experience is, he says, lacking in this 'translation.' What I have just too hastily called 'metaphor' concentrates all the difficulties to come: does one speak 'metaphorically' of the ground for just anything?[35]

The thought of ground-as-support is not just produced by a mistranslation. It is itself no more than a certain account of translation. Translation is understood as presentation of the ground, and mistranslation is understood as loss of support, detachment from ground. The collapse of the tower establishes the necessity of translation as one of reconstruction, edification.[36] Heidegger's account of translation undermines itself when dealing with the translation of the original ground into the idea of the edifice. Heidegger appears to employ an account of translation similar to Derrida's inasmuch as he argues that the violation of the original ground is already there in the Greek original. But then he attempts to go beneath this sense to erase the violation and, in so doing, restores a traditional account of translation. He rebuilds the edifice he appears to have undermined.

Derrida departs from Heidegger precisely by following him. He takes the Heideggerian line further until it folds back on itself, transforming itself. 'Deconstruction' is a 'translation' of two of Heidegger's terms: Destruktion, meaning 'not a destruction but precisely a destructuring that dismantles the structural layers in the systems, and Abbau, meaning 'to take apart an edifice in order to see how it is constituted or deconstituted.'[38] Derrida follows Heidegger's argument that this 'destructuring' or 'unbuilding' disturbs a tradition by inhabiting its structure in a way that exploits its metaphoric resources against itself.

> The movements of deconstruction do not destroy structures from the outside. They are not possible and effective, nor can they take accurate aim, except by inhabiting those structures. Inhabiting them in a certain way, because one always inhabits, and all the more when one does not suspect it. Operating necessarily from the inside, borrowing all the strategic and economic resources of subversion from the old structure, borrowing them structurally . . .'[39]

The concern here is with the way deconstruction inhabits the structure of the edifice, that is, the structure of structure. Deconstruction is neither unbuilding nor demolition. Rather, it is the 'soliciting' of the edifice of metaphysics, the soliciting of structure 'in the sense that Sollicitare, in old Latin means to share as a whole, to make tremble in entirety.' Solicitation is a form of interrogation which shakes structure in order to identify structural weaknesses, weaknesses that are structural.[40]

Derrida destabilises the edifice by arguing that its fundamental condition, its structural possibility, is the concealment of an abyss.

The edifice of metaphysics claims to be stable because it is founded on the bedrock exposed when all the sedimentary layers have been removed. Deconstruction destabilises metaphysics by locating in the bedrock the fractures that undermine its structure. The threat to metaphysics is underground. The subversion of presence is an underground operation. Deconstruction subverts the edifice it inhabits by demonstrating that the ground on which it is erected is insecure: 'the terrain is slippery and shifting, mined and undermined. And this ground is, by essence, an underground'.[41] But the fissures in the ground that crack the structure are not flaws that can be repaired. There is no more stable ground to be found. There is no unflawed bedrock.

Consequently, deconstruction appears to locate in metaphysics the fatal flaw that causes its collapse. It appears to be a form of analysis that dismantles or demolishes structures. It appears to be an undoing of construction. It is in this sense that it is most obviously architectural. But this obvious sense misses the force of deconstruction. Deconstruction is not simply architectural. Rather, it is a displacement of traditional thought about architecture.

> Now the concept of de-construction itself resembles an archi-
> tectural metaphor. It is often said to have a negative attitude.
> Something has been constructed, a philosophical system, a
> tradition, a culture, and along comes a de-constructor and
> destroys it stone by stone, analyses the structure and dissolves
> it. Often enough this is the case. One looks at a system –
> Platonic/Hegellan – and examines how it was built, which
> keystone, which angle of vision supports the authority of the
> system. It seems to me, however, that this is not the essence of
> deconstruction. It is not simply the technique of an architect
> who knows how to de-construct what has been constructed, but
> a probing which touches upon the technique itself, upon the
> authority of the architectural metaphor and thereby constitutes
> its own architectural rhetoric. De-construction is not simply –
> as its name seems to indicate – the technique of a revered
> construction when it is able to conceive for itself the idea of
> construction. One could say that there is nothing more archi-
> tectural than de-construction, but also nothing left architec-
> tural.[42]

Deconstruction leads to a complete rethinking of the supplemental relationship which is organised by the architectural motif on ground/structure/ornament. To disrupt metaphysics in this way is to disrupt the status of architecture. But it is not simply to abandon the traditional architectonic. Rather, it demonstrates that each of its divisions are radically convoluted. Each distinction is made possible by that which is neither one nor the other. The architectural logic of addition is subverted by demonstrating that it is made possible by precisely that which frustrates it.

This subversion of structure does not lead to a new structure. Flaws are identified in the structure but do not lead to its collapse. On the contrary, they are the very source of its strength. Derrida identified the constitutional force of the weakness of a structure, that is, the strength of a certain weakness. Rather than abandoning a structure because its weakness has been found (which would be to remain in complicity with the ideal of a grounded structure), Derrida displaces the architectural motif. Structure becomes 'erected by its very ruin, held up by what never stops eating away at its foundation.'[43] Deconstruction is a form of interrogation that shakes structure in order to identify structural flaws, flaws that are structural. It is not the demolition of particular structures. It displaces the concept of structure itself by locating that which is neither support nor collapse.

> Structure is perceived through the incidence of menace, at the

moment when imminent danger concentrates our vision on the keystone of an institution, the stone which encapsulates both the possibility and the fragility of its existence. Structure then can be methodically threatened in order to be comprehended more clearly and to reveal not only its supports but also that secret place in which it is neither construction nor ruin but liability. This operation is called (from the Latin) soliciting.[44]

The edifice is erected by concealing the abyss on which it stands. This repression produces the appearance of solid ground. The structure does not simply collapse because it is erected on, and fractured by, an abyss. Far from causing its collapse, the fracturing of the ground is the very possibility of the edifice. Derrida identifies the 'structural necessity' of the abyss:

> And we shall see that this abyss is not a happy or unhappy
> accident. An entire theory of the structural necessity of the
> abyss will be gradually constituted in our reading; the indefinite
> process of supplementarity has always already infiltrated pres-
> ence . . . representation in the abyss of presence is not an acci-
> dent of presence; the desire of presence is, on the contrary,
> born from the abyss (the indefinite multiplication) of represen-
> tation, from the representation of the representation, etc.[45]

The abyss is not simply the fracturing of the ground under the edifice. It is the internal fracturing of the edifice, the convolution of the distinction between building and architecture, structure and ornament, presentation and representation. Architecture always already inhabits and underpins the building it is supposedly attached to. It is this convolution that makes possible the thought of a ground that precedes the edifice, a thought that subordinates architecture as merely an addition. Architecture makes possible its own subordination to building.

Deconstruction is concerned with the untranslatable. The remainder that belongs neither to the original nor to the translation, but nevertheless resides within both. Deconstruction marks the structural necessity of a certain failure of translation. That is to say, the structural necessity of architecture. Architecture becomes the possibility of building rather than a simple addition to it. Inasmuch as translation is neither completed nor completely frustrated, the edifice of metaphysics is neither building nor architecture, neither presentation of the ground nor detachment from it, but the uncanny effacement of the distinction between them, the distinction that is at once the contractual possibility of architectural discourse and the means by which to repress the threat posed by that discourse. Deconstruction traces architecture's subversion of building, a subversion that cannot be resisted because architecture is the structural possibility of building. Building always harbours the secret of its constitutional violation by architecture. Deconstruction is the location of that violation. It locates ornament within the structure itself, not by integrating it in some classical synthetic gesture, but, on the contrary, by locating ornament's violation of structure, a violation that cannot he exorcised, a constitutional violation that can only be repressed.

Such a gesture does not constitute a method, a critique, an analysis or a source of legitimation.[46] It is not strategic. It has no prescribed aim, which is not to say that it is aimless. It moves very precisely, but not to some end. It is not a project. It is neither an application of something nor an addition to something. It is, at best, a strange structural condition, an event. It is a displacement of structure that cannot be evaluated in traditional terms because it frustrates the logic of grounding or testing. It is precisely that which is necessary to structure but evades structural analysis (and all analysis is structural): it is the breakdown in structure that is the possibility of structure.

The repression of certain constitutional enigmas is the basis of the social contract which organises the overt discourse. Rather than offering a new account of the architectural object, deconstruction unearths the repressive mechanisms by which that figure of architecture operates. Hidden within the traditional architectural figure is another. The architectural motif is required by philosophy not simply because it is a paradigm of stable structure; it is also required precisely for its instability.

For this reason, to translate deconstruction in architecture is not simply to transform the condition of the architectural object. As metaphysics is the definition of architecture as metaphor, the disruption of architecture's metaphoric condition is a disruption of metaphysics. But this is not to say that this disruption occurs outside the realm of objects. The teleologies of theory/practice, ideal/material, etc. do not disappear. Rather, there is a series of non-linear exchanges within and between these domains, exchanges which 'problematise', but do not abandon, the difference. It is thereby possible to operate within the traditional description of architecture as the representation of structure in order to produce objects which make these enigmas thematic.

Such gestures are neither simply theoretical, nor simply practical. They are neither a new way of reading familiar architecture, nor the means of producing a new architecture. Objects are already bisected into theory and practice. To translate deconstruction in architecture does not lead simply to a formal reconfiguration of the object. Rather, it calls into question the condition of the object, its 'objecthood.' It 'problematises' the condition of the object without simply abandoning it. This is a concern with theoretical objects, objects whose theoretical status and 'objecthood' are problematic, slippery objects that make thematic the theoretical condition of objects and the 'objecthood' of theory.

Such gestures do not simply inhabit the prescribed domains of philosophy and architecture. While philosophical discourse and architectural discourse depend on an explicit account of architecture, they have no unique claim on that account. The translation contract on which those discourses are based underpin a multiplicity of cultural exchanges. The concern becomes the strategic play of the architectural motif in these exchanges. This cultural production of architecture does not take the form specified in architectural discourse; architecture does not occupy the domain allotted to it. Rather than the object of a specific discourse, architecture is a series of discursive mechanisms whose operation has to be traced in ways that are unfamiliar to architectural discourse.

Consequently, the status of the translation of deconstruction in architecture needs to be rethought. A more aggressive reading is required, an architectural transformation of deconstruction that

draws on the gaps in deconstruction that demand such an abuse, sites that already operate with a kind of architectural violence. There is a need for a strong reading which locates that which deconstruction cannot handle of architecture.

Possibilities emerge within architectural discourse that go beyond the displacement of architecture implicit in deconstructive writing. To locate these possibilities is to (re)produce deconstruction by transforming it. Such a transformation must operate on the hesitation deconstruction has about architecture, a hesitation that surfaces precisely within its most confident claims about architecture.

Derrida writes:

> The 'Tower of Babel' does not merely figure the irreducible multiplicity of tongues; it exhibits an incompletion, the impossibility of finishing, of totalising, of saturating, of completing something on the order of edification, architectural construction, system and architectonics. What the multiplicity of idioms actually limits is not only a 'true' translation, a transparent and adequate interexpression, it is also a structural order, a coherence of construct. There is then (let us translate) something like an internal limit to formalisation, an incompleteness of the constructure. It would be easy and up to a certain point justified to see there the translation of a system in deconstruction.[47]

This passage culminates symptomatically in a sentence that performs the classical philosophical gesture. Architecture is at once given constitutive power and has that power frustrated by returning its status to mere metaphor. Here the tower, the figure of translation, is itself understood as a translation, the architectural translation of deconstruction. Which, in Derridean terms, is to say a figure that does not simply represent deconstruction, but is its possibility. But an inquiry needs to focus on why an architectural reading of deconstruction is 'easy' and what is the 'certain point' beyond which it becomes unjustified, improper. A patient reading needs to force the convoluted surface of deconstructive writing and expose the architectural motif within it.

But perhaps even such an abusive reading of Derrida is insufficient. In as much as deconstruction is abused in architectural discourse, its theory of translation, which is to say its theory of abuse, needs to be rethought. Because of architecture's unique relationship to translation, it cannot simply translate deconstruction. It is so implicated in the economy of translation that it threatens deconstruction. There is an implicit identity between the untranslatable remainder located by deconstruction and that part of architecture that causes deconstruction to hesitate the architecture it resists. Consequently, deconstruction does not simply survive architecture.

The text was first given as a paper at the Chicago Institute for Architecture and Urbanism conference on 'Theory' in August 1988.

Notes

1 Jacques Derrida, *Positions*, trans Alan Bass (Chicago: University of Chicago Press, 1981), 20.

2 'A text lives only if it lives on (*sur-vit*), and it lives *on* only if it is at once translatable and untranslatable . . . Totally translatable, it disappears as a text, as writing, as a body of language (*langue*). Totally untranslatable, even within what is believed to be one language, it dies immediately. Thus triumphant translation is neither the life nor the death of the text, only or already its living on, its life after life, its life after death.'
Jacques Derrida, 'Living On: Border Lines', trans James Hulbert, in *Deconstruction and Criticism* (New York: Seabury Press,

1979), 102.

3 Cf. Jacques Derrida, 'Me – Psychoanalysis: An Introduction to *The Shell and the Kernel* by Nicolas Abraham,' trans Richard Klein, *Diacritics* (Spring 1979).

4 Deconstruction is considered here in the context of philosophy. While Derrida repeatedly argues that deconstruction is not philosophy, he also notes that it is not non-philosophy either. To simply claim that deconstruction is not philosophy is to maintain philosophy by appealing to its own definition of its other. It is to participate in the dominant reading of Derrida that resists the force of deconstruction. That force is produced by identify-

ing the complicity of the apparently non-philosophical within the philosophical tradition. Deconstruction occupies the texts of philosophy in order to identify a non-philosophical site within them. Deconstruction cannot be considered outside the texts of philosophy it inhabits, even as a foreigner.

5 'For if the difficulties of translation can be anticipated . . . one should not reign by naively believing that the word *deconstruction* corresponds in French to some clear and univocal signification. There is already in *my* language a serious (*sombre*) problem of translation between what here or there can be envisaged for the word, and the usage itself, the reserves of the word. Jacques Derrida, 'Letter to a Japanese Friend', in *Derrida and Difference*, ed David Wood and Robert Bernasconi (Coventry: Parousia Press, 1985), 1.

6 Immanuel Kant, *Critique of Pure Reason*, trans Norman Kemp Smith (London: MacMillan and Co., 1929) 47.

7 Ibid, 608.

8 Ibid, 14.

9 Ibid, 219.

10 Martin Heidegger, *An Introduction to Metaphysics*, trans John Macquarrie and Edward Robinson (New York, Harper and Row, 1962), 2.

11 Cf the Greek temple in 'The Origin of the Work of Art': 'Truth happens in the temple's standing where it is. This does not mean that something is correctly represented and rendered there, but that what is as a whole is brought into unconcealedness and held therein.' Martin Heidegger, 'The origin of the Work of Art', in *Poetry, Language, Thought*, trans Albert Hofstadter (New York: Harper and Row, 1971). The edifice is neither a representation of the ground, nor even a presentation, but is the production of the world.

12 '(I)t is precisely the idea that it is a matter of providing a foundation for an edifice already constructed that must be avoided.' Martin Heidegger, *Kant and the Problem of Metaphysics*, trans James S Churchill (Bloomington: Indiana University Press, 1962), 4.

13 '(T)he foundation of traditional metaphysics shaken and the edifice . . . begins to totter.' Ibid, 129.

14 Immanuel Kant, *Critique of Pure Reason*, 60.

15 Martin Heidegger, *Kant and the Problem of Metaphysics*, 5.

16 Jacques Derrida, 'Structure, Sign and Play in the Discourse of the Human Sciences,' in *Writing and Difference*, trans Alan Bass (Chicago: University of Chicago Press, 1978) 279.

17 Martin Heidegger, 'The Origin of the Work of Art,' 19.

18 Jacques Derrida 'Parergoni', in *Truth in Painting*, trans Geoff Bennington and Ian McCleod Alan Bass (Chicago: University of Chicago Press, 1987) 40.

I9 Jacques Derrida, 'Force and Signification', in *Writing and Difference*, 17.

20 Ibid, 27.

21 Jacques Derrida, 'White Mythology: Metaphor in the Text of Philosophy', in *Margins of Philosophy*, trans Alan Bass (Chicago: University of Chicago Press, 1982) 224.

22 Not in the sense of the structuralist concern for architecture as a kind of language, a system of objects to which language theory can be applied, but as the possibility of thought about language.

23 'With this problem of translation we will thus be dealing with nothing less than the problem of the very passage into philosophy.' Jacques Derrida, *Dissemination*, trans Barbara Johnson (Chicago: University of Chicago Press, 1981) 72.

24 'Had their enterprise succeeded, the universal tongue would have been a particular language imposed by violence, by force. It would not have been a universal language – for example in the Leibnizian sense – a transparent language to which everyone would have access. 'Jacques Derrida, *The Ear of the Other*, ed Christie V McDonald (New York: Schocken Books, 1985), 101 Cf Jacques Derrida, 'Languages and the Institutions of Philosophy', *Recherche et Semiotique/Semiotic Inquiry*, vol.4 no.2 (1984): 91-154. on the violent imposition of language.

25 '(A)nd the question of deconstruction is also through and through the question of translation . . .' Jacques Derrida, 'Letter to a Japanese Friend', 6.

26 Jacques Derrida, *The Ear of the Other*, 102.

27 Jacques Derrida, 'Architecture Where the Desire May Live,' *Domus* 671 (1986): 25.

28 Jacques Derrida, 'Des Tours de Babel,' trans Joseph F Graham (Ithaca: Cornell university Press, 1985), 184.

29 Ibid, 182.

30 Martin Heidegger *An Introduction to Metaphysics*, 93.

31 This degenerate translation is based on a degeneration that already occurred within the original Greek, requiring a return to a more primordial origin: 'But With this Latin translation the original meaning of the Greek word is destroyed. This is true not only of the Latin translation of this word but of all other Roman translations of the Greek philosophical language. What happened in this translation from the Greek into the Latin is not accidental and harmless; it marks the first stage in the process by which we cut ourselves off and alienates ourselves from the original essence of Greek philosophy . . . But it should be said in passing that even within Greek philosophy a narrowing of the word set in forthwith, although the original meaning did not vanish from the experience, knowledge, and orientation of Greek philosophy.' Martin Heidegger, *An Introduction to Metaphysics*, 13.

32 'The perfection of technology is only the echo of the claim to the . . . completeness of the foundation . . . Thus the characteristic domination of the principle of ground then determines the essence of our modern technological age.' Martin Heidegger, 'The Principle of Ground,' *Man and World* 7, trans Keith Hoeller (1974), 213.

33 Ibid, 204.

34 Martin Heidegger, 'Building, Dwelling, Thinking,' in *Poetry, Language, Thought*, 159.

35 Jacques Derrida, 'Restitutions of the Truth in Painting,' in *The Truth in Painting*, 290.

36 Note how Derrida argues that the university is 'built' on the ideal of translation (Jacques Derrida, 'Living On; Border Line,' 93-94) in the same way that he argues that it is 'built' on the ideal of ground-as-support (Jacques Derrida, 'The University in the Eyes of Reason,' *Diacritics* (Fall 1983) 11-20).

37 '*Beneath* the seemingly literal and thus faithful translation there is concealed . . . a translation without a corresponding, equally authentic experience of what they say. The rootlessness of Western thought begins with this translation.' Martin Heidegger, 'The Origin of the Work of Art,' 23 (emphasis added). 'We are not merely taking refuge in a more literal translation of a Greek word. We are reminding ourselves of what, inexperienced and unthought, *underlies* our familiar and therefore outworn essence of truth . . .' ibid 52 (emphasis added).

38 Jacques Derrida, 'Roundtable on Autobiography,' trans Peggy Kamuf in *The Ear of the Other*, 86. Of the word 'deconstruction': 'Among other things I wished to translate and adapt to my own ends the Heideggerian word *Destruktion* or *Abbau*. Each signified in this context an operation bearing on the structure or traditional architecture of the fundamental concept of ontology or of western metaphysics.' Jacques Derrida, 'Letter to a Japanese Friend,' 1.

39 Jacques Derrida, *Of Grammatology*, trans Gayatri Chakravorty Spivak (Baltimore: Johns Hopkins Press, 1976) 24.

40 Jacques Derrida, 'Difference', in *Margins of Philosophy*, 21.

41 Jacques Derrida, *Limited Inc.*, (Baltimore: John Hopkins University Press, 1977) 168.

42 Jacques Derrida, 'Architecture where the Desire May Live.'

43 Jacques Derrida, 'Force', trans Barbara Johnson, *The Georgia Review* 31 no.I (1977), 40.

44 Jacques Derrida, 'Force and Signification,' 6.

45 Jacques Derrida, *Of Grammatology*, 163.

46 '(I)n spite of appearances, deconstruction is neither an *analysis* nor a *critique* and its translation would have to take that into consideration. It is not an analysis in particular because the dismantling of a structure is not a regression towards a *simple* element, towards an *indissoluble origin*. These values, like that of analysis, are themselves philosophemes subject to deconstruction'. Jacques Derrida, 'Letter to a Japanese Friend,' 4.

47 Jacques Derrida, 'Des Tours de Babel,' 165.

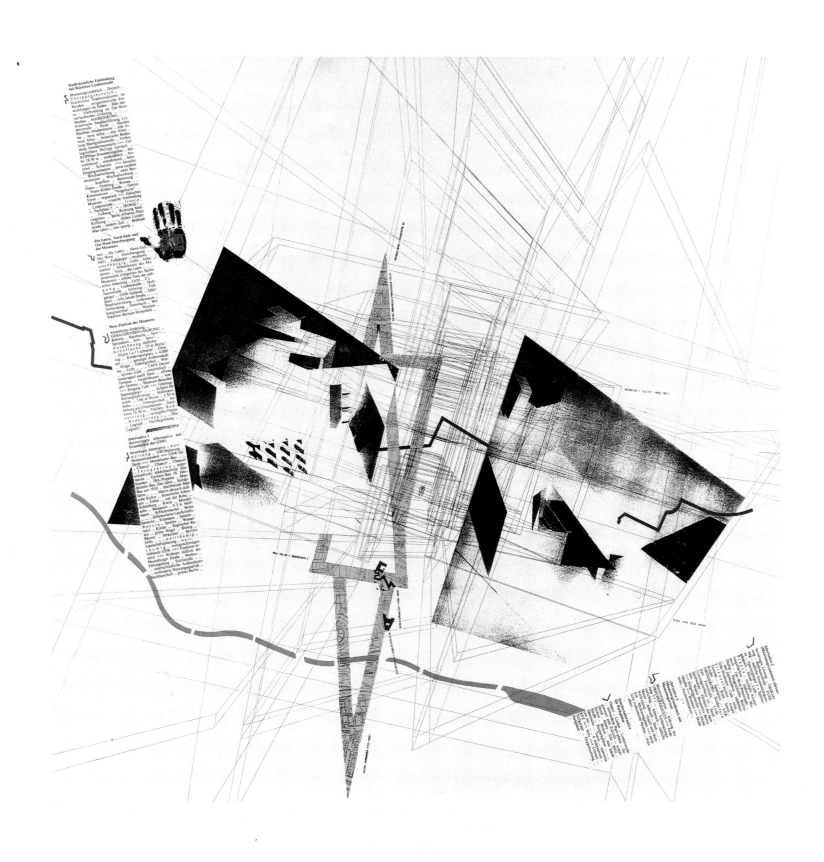

THE JEWISH EXTENSION TO THE BERLIN MUSEUM

DANIEL LIBESKIND
AN ARCHITECTURAL DESIGN INTERVIEW

– Could you, first of all, tell me a little about your background?

I was born in Poland and went to school there. My family then emigrated to Israel. I studied to be a musician and won the American-Israel Cultural Foundation Fellowship in 1960 so I went to study in New York. In fact, I won the fellowship together with Isaac Perleman. I was a virtuoso performer for a while but I gave it up. . . despite the advice of Isaac Stern. I gave it up for one simple reason: there was no more 'technique' I could acquire. . . so what was the point of playing? I then turned to architecture, a field whose 'technique' seemed so simple in comparison to music there would never be a problem of its ultimate exhaustion.

My architectural education was at Cooper Union where I first met John Hejduk and Peter Eisenman who inspired me to study architecture. After graduating from Cooper Union I read, studied, thought and taught. I read extensively, studied history and philosophy, thought about the relation between words and lines and taught – as a Unit Master at the Architectural Association and in a number of other schools. Subsequently, I was involved in teaching Architecture as Head of the Department at Cranbrook and later as Founder and Director of Architecture Intermundium – which I founded as an alternative to both 'theory and practice'. Architecture Intermundium was and continues to be an attempt to get away from existing methods of production and discourse in the field – in short, to 'de-institutionalise' architectural thought. Architecture Intermundium is actually modelled after alchemical laboratories of the early Renaissance where no distinction was of yet made between magic, symbolism, ritual and technology; that is between being and non-being.

– I wanted to ask you particularly about your Jewish sense, especially with you having lived in Israel and then both in the United States and Europe.

I feel that if one is Jewish, one doesn't really have a place anywhere. Of course, this sense of Jewishness is not a matter of choice.

– It is something that you can try to get away from, however.

I myself came from a secular background. My immediate family background is rabbinical on one side, anarchist on the other. So my own sense of Jewishness has nothing to do with either fundamentalism or rebellion.

– Do you see a difference, again having lived both in America and Europe, between Jewish intellect in the United States and that of Europe?

That's a difficult question to answer. I think there is more vitality in North America whereas in Europe the community tends to be more conservative. Obviously it depends on the person and the place. . . To the extent that America cannot exist without Europe or Europe cannot exist without America, the same could also be said about the Jewish communities; they need each other for various reasons.

– When you were describing the Berlin City Edge Competition, you talked about using the block structure of the city whilst attempting to transcend the physical limitations of the structure. Could you explain this a little further?

As you know, the IBA master plan had to do with blocks of the city and with certain heights of buildings. The idea was to re-establish some sort of block structure, the urban structure of the city. However, there are various possibilities of how one relates to this urban structure; one can also say that *not* relating is a form of relationship as well. In terms of the actual project, I used the block structure in a very precise urban, geometric and functional way. The building of the City Edge had to do with, for example, the average height of buildings – even though one end of the building was high up over the city and the other end was sunk and

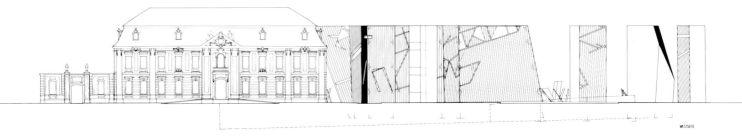

buried within the block. On average, therefore, technically, the height was exactly the height of Berlin, although it was not taken as a parallel line running from roof-line to roof-line. This is just a small illustration to say that I used the block structure not as given but as an on-going discourse so that whatever one finds archaeologically in the structure is not necessarily what the structure implies. On the one hand, there is the archaeology of the structure – the remnants, the ruins – while on the other hand, there are developments that have very little to do with what one finds; reality comes from elsewhere – not from the physical structure itself. However, it's not an abstract, hypothetical manner of dealing with the block. It *is* dealing with the block pragmatically yet with other goals. I used one part of the block as a hinge-point or fulcrum – with which to alter the second block – which was much more devastated and empty. Consequently, you can see that there are many different functions of the block: not just housing but industry, public places and facilities. My idea was not to reconstruct a homogeneous facade behind which all these contradictions work but to offer each functional aspect of the city a spiritual situation within an overall structure.

– How confining is the physical space? Can the architect transcend it, or can he play with it, exploiting the trap of the space?

I think one should not be too impressed by what is called 'physical space.' Physical space is good for physics; it's not an architectural space and it's interesting that most architects still talk about architecture as if it were founded in physics – not just Euclidean physics but also the physics of building. It's clear that a building is not just made out of glass and bricks – even if it *is* made from these materials – but is constituted by something else. It might be *founded* on these hierarchies of material reality but that would be to say that human beings were based on fish or protozoa; of course they are, but there is a difference between foundation and *formation*. And to the extent that architecture is to do with formative reality, not just foundational reality, one could not deal with architecture as being bound by physics – especially physics of the Enlightenment – which, when you think about it, is what architects really do. Even if they want to destroy that space, they often use the same techniques that were used in the classical notion of the world to constitute it. To answer your question briefly is difficult because it concerns what is given in architecture; but I would say that what is given is not a physical reality: it is a relationship to something that is both immanent in physical reality but not apparent in something which goes beyond it as well. At the same time, 'givenness' has to do with desire. If anything is important to architecture it is the field which incorporates these tendencies, not an *object*. There is a very beautiful quotation by Malevich where he says, 'What is a car? There are no cars in Moscow as a car is just a bunch of gears and things put together.' The notion of the car is very different from the car they had in Moscow.

– In Between the Lines, *when you are explaining the Jewish Extension in Berlin, you speak about 'flexible spaces with open narratives.' Don't you, however, think that a narrative is more a closed structure, so it allows room for the viewer, or museum-goer, to 'breathe,' interpreting the collection as he is walking through the space. Nevertheless, he is* within *the space, caught up in it. The collection, however, is static – it is viewed and is there to be*

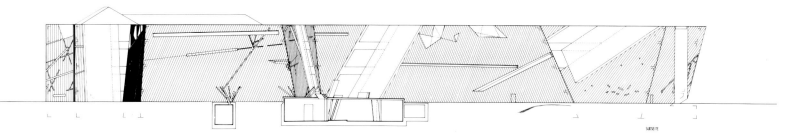

viewed – with the museum-goer moving, looking and interpreting but only *within the space of the museum. How open – or rather 'unclosed' – can a narrative be?*

I used the word 'narrative' in a very guarded way in the sense that there will always be a story to be told about the works one has seen in a museum. The point about the *open* narrative is that the various stories one can make about the museum are at odds with each other and also cannot be reconciled by any overall thematic because the narrative, as you say, exists in a balanced field of contention. For example, the narrative of the absent space is not more dominant than the narrative of the space which continues across this absence. In a way, what I'm trying to do is to make sure that the people who go to the museum have a chance to distance themselves from the collection in the Berlin museum in order to be engaged in the collection in a completely different manner. Then it has to do with how one disposes and organises the collection. For example, relative to the Void, I've tried to suggest that the presence of those citizens of Berlin who are also absent cannot easily be discriminated into two different yet reconcilable sets – the Jewish collection and the Berlin collection belong simultaneously with all their contradictions across both collections and are to be found in neither. The wall of the void has two sides – one is seen from a continuous access through the museum and the other is seen when you come into the void, as if it were exterior to the building; this wall, or doubling of the wall, is meant also to suggest ways in which to exhibit works. For example, you could have a situation where you see the back of an object from the front of the space and see the front of the object from the edge of the space, the marginal space. That, I think, would be appropriate to show the ambivalence, ambiguity and, ultimately, the difficulty of integration, and retrospective integration at that.

– You talk about absent space and absent space exists, but I always wonder how difficult it is for an architect to actually put this absence into practice.

It is difficult because whatever absence there is it is not found in the world. In the world, we find only the impossibility of finding that absence. And *that* absence is manifested in the presence of building as a built-in absence. It's constructed – but that is not to say that it is not there. This can be seen in the way a grave or a pyramid is constructed. Think of the many centuries of social effort to construct pyramids which were to be used after dying only by one person. It's a matter of orientation and also of faith and belief. We should not underestimate these criteria for architecture just because people do not talk about them today.

– I notice that the title for the museum in Berlin is the Jewish Extension to the Berlin Museum. The word 'extension' struck me as I read that title; it seemed to me as if it were moving towards ghettoising the Jews by putting the collection in an 'extension'.

You've hit on a very interesting point. Think about what it means to 'extend' the Berlin museum with a Jewish museum. The museum is the place of the Muses – the Muse of Berlin is guarding Berlin history. To extend this Musical relationship across a gap which would then constitute the Jewish museum is a fascinating idea. If you use the word 'extend' you are obviously not simply putting in another element, a foreign element, that could be ghettoising. How can you extend Berlin history with Jewish history? It is a very provocative theme because you cannot extend simply by elaborating Berlin history to its tragic finale in the

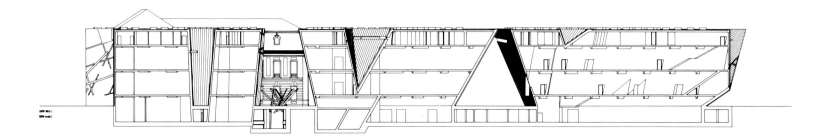

Holocaust, but neither can you extend it by treating the Jewish collection as if it were just another contribution beneath the umbrella of the Berlin museum. This is the problematic hidden in the idea of the disaster to which this museum is related and which I find very interesting. And now we are totally in the realm of the spiritual. . . At a casual glance it might seem that to extend it with the Jewish museum would be just to add on to it; to supplement it with its own absence or its own missing self. But to take truly the challenge of *extension* of Berlin history right to and through the absolute event – not a relative event as it is not relative to Berlin's history, because beyond it nothing can happen in that direction that has not already happened – is something that I took very seriously, trying to stay away from any simple notion of adding or subtracting another building. I don't know whether it answers your question; it only opens the question further. . . Concentrating on the word 'extension' for a moment, as in to extend an arm, or 'to extend one's grasp or reach', is very different from extending the hand in physical terms with a prosthetic device. And that's the difference in the articulation of extension. There were architects in the competition who extended the museum by adding on to it; I extended it by hollowing its underground or its underworldly possibilities, in an openness which is not particularly connected with the apparent space of the Berlin Museum as it exists today.

– Is there a Jewish collection already housed in the Berlin Museum?

There is a Jewish collection which belongs to Berlin. I find the collection very interesting as it is an incredibly poignant remnant of a community which, because of its integration with German history and society, did not particularly busy itself with its own lack of identity; the Jewish community in Berlin was a very assimilated yet coherent community. So what remains is, in itself, a sign that has to be interpreted; it's not a sign that points to a *type* of Jewishness, be it religious or whatever. It is a sign that is not a last sign either. Therefore, there exists the functional problem: how to exhibit these things; what are these signs pointing to; would someone get an idea of Jewish history by looking at these signs; what does the viewer see?

– Earlier, you spoke about the void in relation to the narrative of absent space which can suggest ways of exhibiting in a museum. I am interested in your choosing to call it the 'Void.' Could you tell me about your use of this word which is also a built space?

Yes. There is a Void in the building that is built as a space but the use of which is precisely in its uselessness, ie it is not used as a normal museum space in which to put normal museum objects. Putting that word in the museum vocabulary makes people more aware that there is another manner of building – how that word relates to the entire notion of architecture and how one conceives of it in relation to architecture.

– How does the Void then generate desire; or is the desire there already, allowing the Void to exist?

It's a difficult question to answer. The void is there because you cross it and yet cannot get to it; but had the void been there without one's awareness of it then it would cease to be a void – it would simply not be there. All these very subtle meanings are not really intellectual; they are carnal. At which point is a trajectory that goes nowhere seen as negative and at

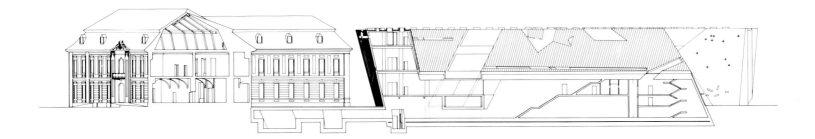

which point does it become a very meaningful form of desire? You're crossing a space which, unlike a normal galleria, does not lead you to a collection; a passage which doesn't lead you to show you the goods of the museum. There *is* a passage but it doesn't get you anywhere; it doesn't show the museum as an attractive entity in that sense. It appears, however, as you walk through it, that you understand more about what is *not* being shown by what you have seen as not being able to be shown.

– In your talk at The New Moderns Symposium at the Tate Gallery in September, you spoke about the irrational matrix at the Extension, the form of which would yield some reference to the emblematics of a distorted star of David. How does the form of the star of David, a distorted star of David, add to the significance of the Extension (without being overtly obvious)? Does it really contribute towards an understanding of Jewish history?

I attempted to project the star of David from the city in order to provide myself with the distorted geometry which would relate itself to that particular 'yellow' of the undistorted Jewish star worn all over Berlin (and everywhere else in Europe) and also the strange yellow cover of Schoenberg's *Moses and Aaron*, published so incredibly as no. 8004 Edition Eulenburg. The significance, for me, of this act is two-fold: first, this geometry remains dominant over what has been erased by being invisibly built into a non-existent context. Second, it does contribute to the understanding of Jewish history precisely by refusing to enter the visible realm of monumental civic space where the embodiment of geometry becomes its death. Here the museum-goer is aware of the gap which separates the physiognomy of the building from the shape of the soul – which, according to the Jewish tradition, is not closed but opens itself towards non-spatial realms.

– There is an obvious musicality and rhythm in your writings. How do you personally attain this in your built projects? You quoted Schoenberg's 'inaudible music' in your piece Between the Lines.

I worked very closely with Schoenberg's score *Moses and Aaron*. It is also a very interesting piece of architecture because Schoenberg's structure, as you know, was designed around the ramification of harmonics as they are transformed into another system by exhausting their own capacity for relationships – thus dissolving the old notion of harmony and also attaining the 'inaudible' aspects of relations. 'Inaudible' in the sense that it is the voice of conscience and grace in human existence. I literally tried to make the space in the museum proportional to the rhythm of the non-existent Act Three. This has a lot to do with *Moses and Aaron*; not only because Moses and Aaron adds up to twelve letters, and forms a hermetic twelve-tone system of Schoenberg, but because it deals with the impossibility of extending that attitude to music, art and culture through Schoenberg's reading of Berlin. He converted to Protestantism when young as many Jews did, and in 1933, when the Aryan biological and racial laws came into effect, he reconverted back to Judaism. . . But as for music and architecture, one should rather say architecture is already music. . . even when the music is inaudible.

FRANK GEHRY
THE VITRA DESIGN MUSEUM

The Vitra Design Museum, in Weil am Rhein, Germany, is the first European commission by Frank Gehry. Below we present this highly-acclaimed building together with statements by the Director of the Museum, the Managing Director of Vitra and the architect.

Alexander von Vegesack

The point of departure for the idea of the Vitra Design Museum was the existence of a collection of international furniture design objects. From there came the wish to explore the history and future development of this discipline.

The museum's purpose is to pass on the knowledge and experience gained in this process to the interested visitor. Our objective here is to offer the information in a way that can be directly experienced to satisfy both playful curiosity and serious research. The exhibitions are planned such that the design creation process becomes understandable in all of its stages of development.

Historical themes, alternating with current and future trends, will be made more accessible with the help of key objects.

The museum's layout allows up to three different concurrent exhibitions, in different rhythms. Thus objects from the museum's own collections as well as exhibitions from outside or organised in cooperation with other museums can be displayed at the same time, under changing aspects.

Although the thematic focus is on furniture, museum activities will also deal with themes reaching beyond interior decoration to include space and architecture. Inquiries of this sort might take painting, photography, design, crafts or sociological issues as their starting point.

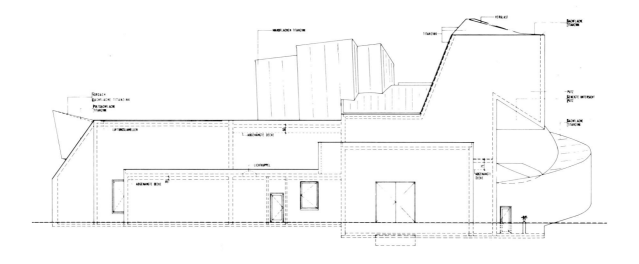

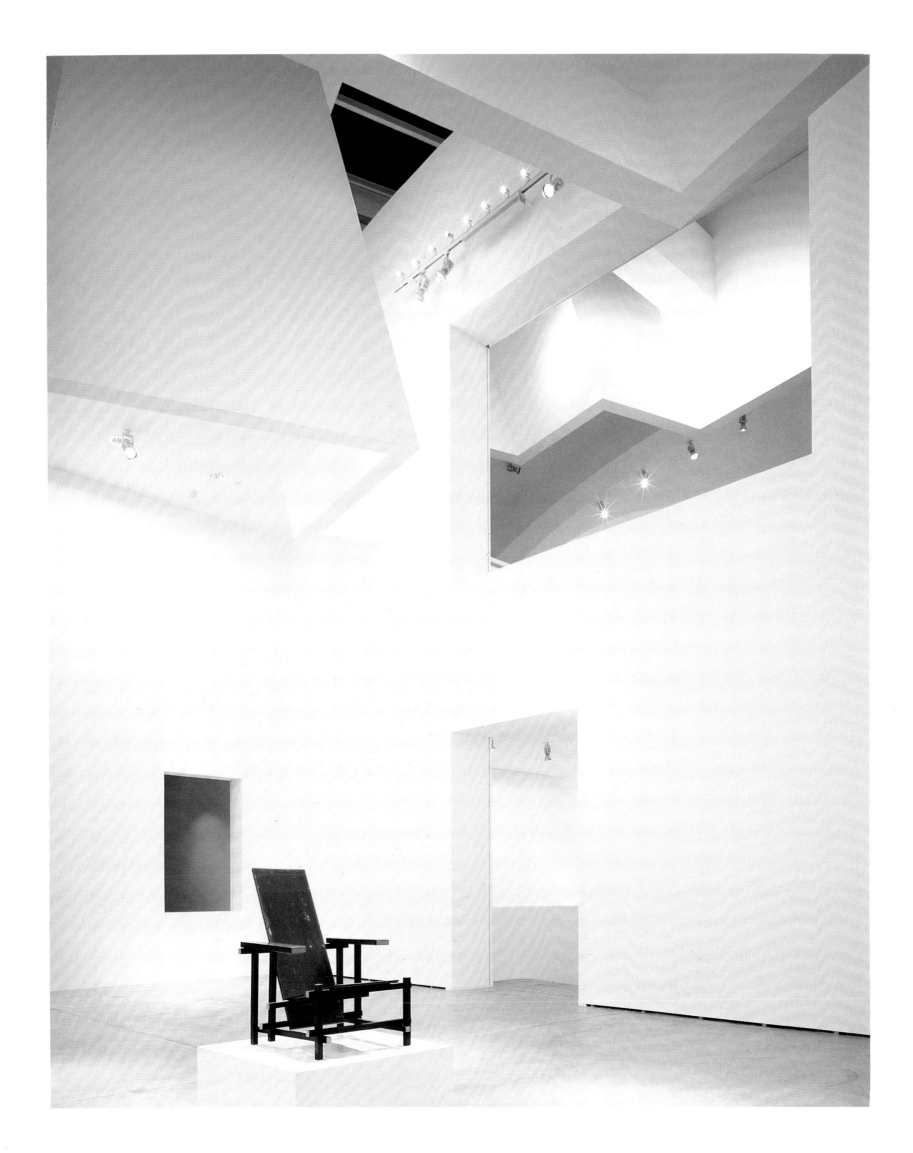

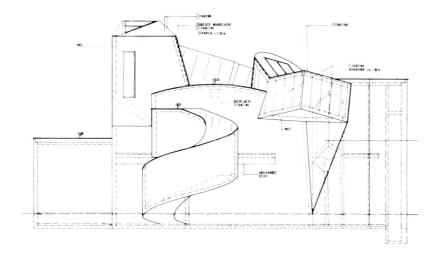

Rolf Fehlbaum

A chair is a fascinating creature. There is no other object of everyday life, except one's clothes, to which Western man is so closely attached. Like us, it has legs, arms, a seat and a back. It supports our body and invites us to relax. At the same time, it stands for our status (for example a throne).

A chair is always the same as far as its basic structure is concerned – the vertical line of its legs and back and the horizontal line of its seat. Nevertheless, it is always different because it is a precise expression of the Zeitgeist. This combination of similarity in structure and difference in expression raises the interest in a chair as a collection object.

Vitra's collection activities started with the discovery of lost witnesses of our own production – such as models of Eames and Nelson. Today, the museum accommodates more than 1,200 chairs and other furniture pieces. It establishes documentary evidence of the development of industrially produced furniture from the middle of the 19th century until today.

The Vitra Design Museum is an homage to the great designers and the vital phenomenon of design. Design is neither applied art nor reduced architecture but a new autonomous discipline which came to fruition only in this century. Therefore, for Vitra, it goes without saying that orders for building tasks are placed only with innovative architects.

We started our conscious building activities in 1981 with the English high-tech architect Nicholas Grimshaw. The buildings of Frank Gehry form a good contrast to those of Grimshaw. Because every single building activity, even the smallest, represents a creative chance, annexes and structural alterations were also planned by qualified architects like Eva Jiricna from London and Antonio Citterio from Milan. At the moment a fire station is planned by Zaha Hadid and a conference pavilion by Tadao Ando.

This pluralism in architecture is, in contrast to the usual ideas of a uniform architecture, part of the corporate identity. Since Vitra also offers a broad spectrum of products – from the classic via the progressive mainstream to the avant-garde – it is only adequate to choose a pluralistic attempt in architecture.

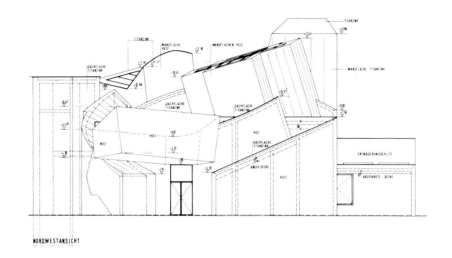

NORDWESTANSICHT

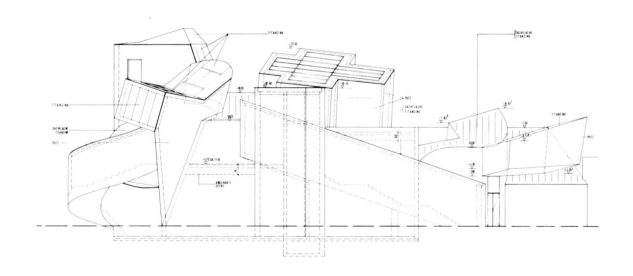

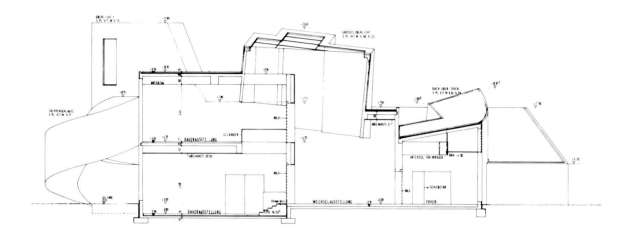

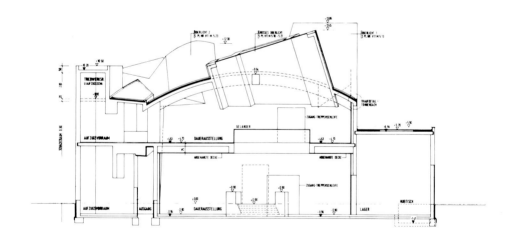

29

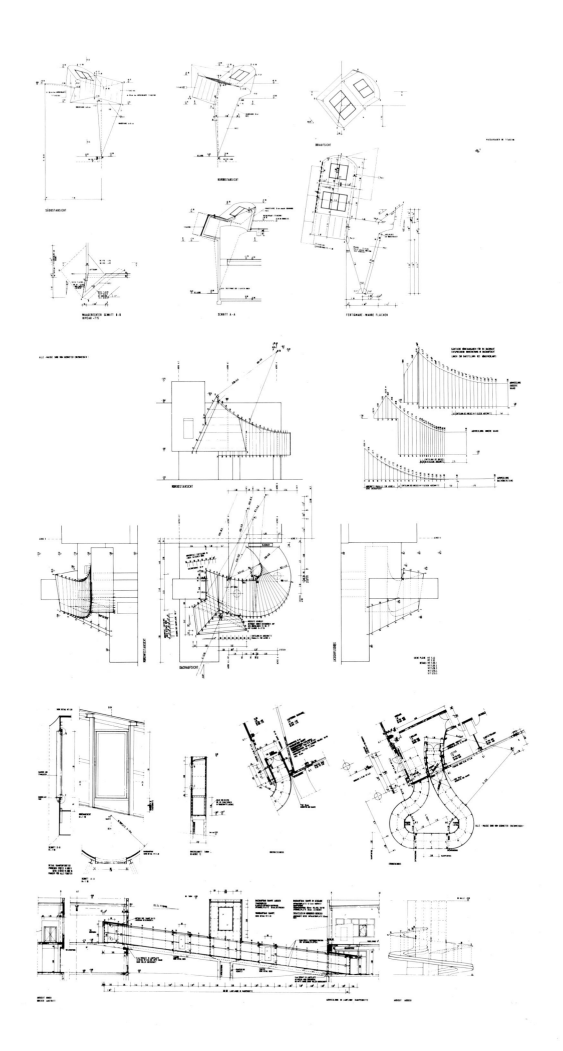

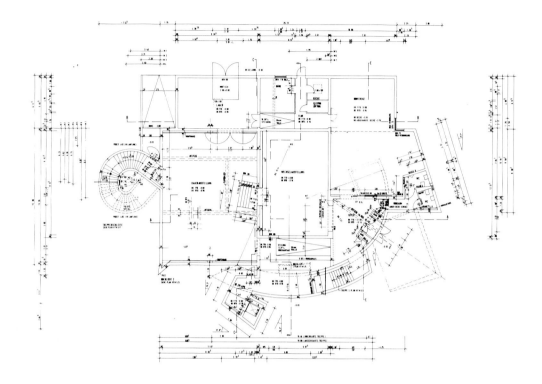

Frank Gehry

This project encompasses three major parts: a seating assembly plant with an adjacent office; mezzanine and distribution areas; and a small furniture museum to house a collection of furniture (19th century through to today) as well as a library and preparation of a master plan for this project, which also includes a new entrance road and gate-house, a future expansion of the factory, museum parking and ancillary facilities.

The factory is a concrete frame construction with a stucco finish, skylights and large windows. The offices located on the north mezzanine have spectacular views of the adjacent hills as well as of the museum and a Claes Oldenburg sculpture. This north facade faces the main factory and serves as a backdrop for the museum. Ramps and entrance canopies flank this factory facade and make sculptural 'book-ends' to the museum. These forms relate to each other and extend the visual impact of the project as a whole. They are the sculptural elements which gave scale to the big, simple, factory volume, and they add to the campus-like environment. A consistent, albeit differentiated, formal vocabulary ties the various pieces together as one moves through and around the buildings. Skylights and clerestories create various natural lighting conditions within these forms.

The museum building is composed of a catalogue library, office, storage and support spaces in addition to exhibition space. The galleries are treated as connected volumes which interpenetrate each other so that the exhibitions can communicate from one space to another. Each has a different character vis-à-vis natural light, volume, surface and scale and although visually connected, they may all be secured separately.

Natural light is introduced from skylights which are shaped to bounce and diffuse it. This softens the light such that at times the space simply glows. The construction is plaster over masonry on vertical and inverted surfaces and metal roofing panels on sloped water shedding surfaces. White plaster with titan zinc seem appropriate materials for this area.

The master plan calls for several independent galleries to be added to the initial museum building and for additional factories to be added to the west side of the new entrance road. Parking is eventually to be expanded at the west and south ends of the site.

BERNARD TSCHUMI
ZENTRUM FÜR KUNST UND MEDIENTECHNOLOGIE, KARLSRUHE
Competition Entry

At the end of the 20th century, the condition of architecture and urbanism is undergoing profound changes that are closely intertwined with the broader questions of society, its art and its technology. Karlsruhe and its new Centre for Art and Media Technology ZKM are characteristic of that condition, which solicits the following four enquiries:

1 How can the boundaries of an historically centralised, pre-industrial city survive their inescapable transformation into a non-centralised, post-industrial 21st century territory: **how can limits be turned into lines of exchange?**

2 How can institutions dedicated to specialised research and to the development of ideas simultaneously provide information and excitement to a larger public: **how can the public mediate specialised research?**

3 How can one construct a building at a time when the technology of construction has become less relevant than **the construction of technology?**

4 How can architecture, whose historical role was to generate the appearance of stable images (monuments, order, etc) deal with today's culture of **the disappearance of unstable images** (24 image per second cinema, video and computer-generated images)?
   Our proposal for the new Centre ZKM reflects these four questions through the projects' four components: the urban line of exchange, the linear core, the two compartments and the casing.

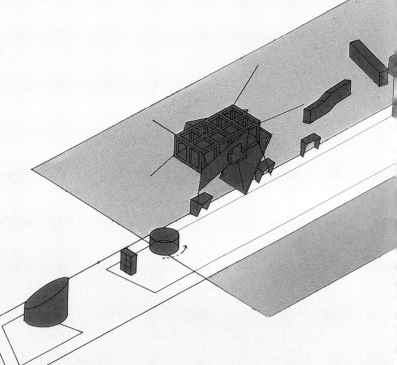

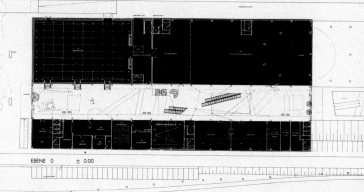

EBENE 0   ± 0.00

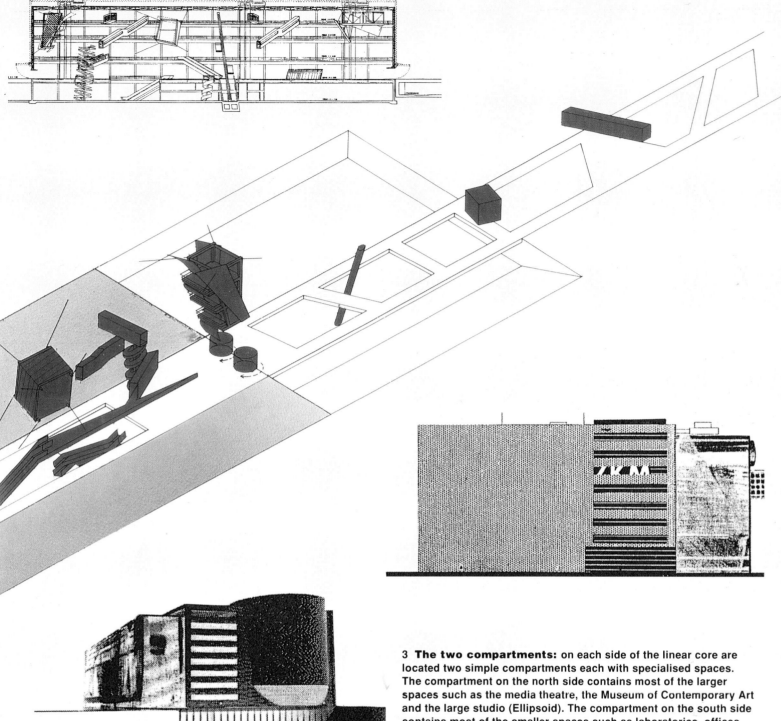

1 The urban line of exchange: we suggest a new linear public passage of intense interchange and communication as an alternative to the concentric Baroque Karlsruhe. This line is aimed at providing a new urban system at the historical edge of the city by turning the old limit into **a new line of exchange.**
(Note: the underground passage through the railway station is animated by banks of closed-circuit television monitors controlled by ZKM.)

2 The linear core: at the centre of the building, we propose a linear public space of maximum visibility and excitement. This linear core and its balconies give access to all parts of the ZKM. Its ground floor serves most performances, exhibitions and seminar spaces. Giant video screens, suspended passerelles and stairs, a tensile glass elevator and two rooms floating in mid-air activate an extensive and colourful foyer for the general public. This linear core allows for **the public mediatisation of specialised research.**

3 The two compartments: on each side of the linear core are located two simple compartments each with specialised spaces. The compartment on the north side contains most of the larger spaces such as the media theatre, the Museum of Contemporary Art and the large studio (Ellipsoid). The compartment on the south side contains most of the smaller spaces such as laboratories, offices and artists' studios, as well as the media gallery. On both sides, the more public spaces are located on the lower floors and the more specialised spaces on the upper floors.

The functional and constructive systems of the two compartments are kept intentionally simple: repetitive cells on a regular concrete structure. The building's simplicity and sobriety is meant to suggest that at ZKM emphasis is placed on the development of new media, on **the construction of technology** (rather than on the technology of construction).

4 The casing: the tight functional structure is enclosed on the south side by an everchanging, photo-electronic, computer-animated, double-glazed skin that can react to external light and sound variations. The skin is seen to emerge from a solid, protective, perforated, stainless steel enclosure (north side), with a copper-clad ellipsoid (containing the multi-purpose studio).

The digitised facade of the casing reminds us that if, once upon a time, architecture generated the appearance of stable images, today it may reveal **the transience of unstable images.**

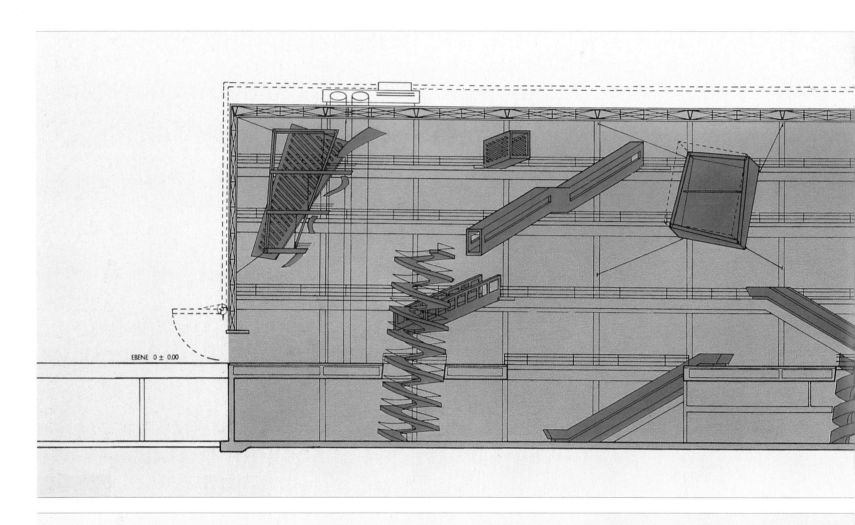

EBENE 0 ± 0.00

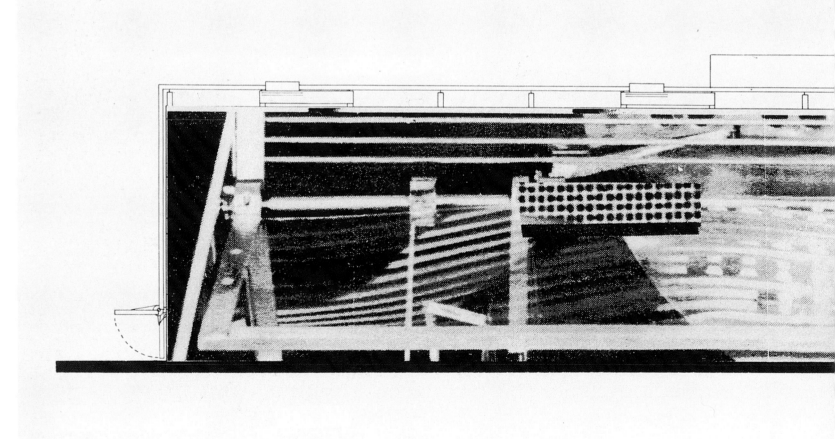

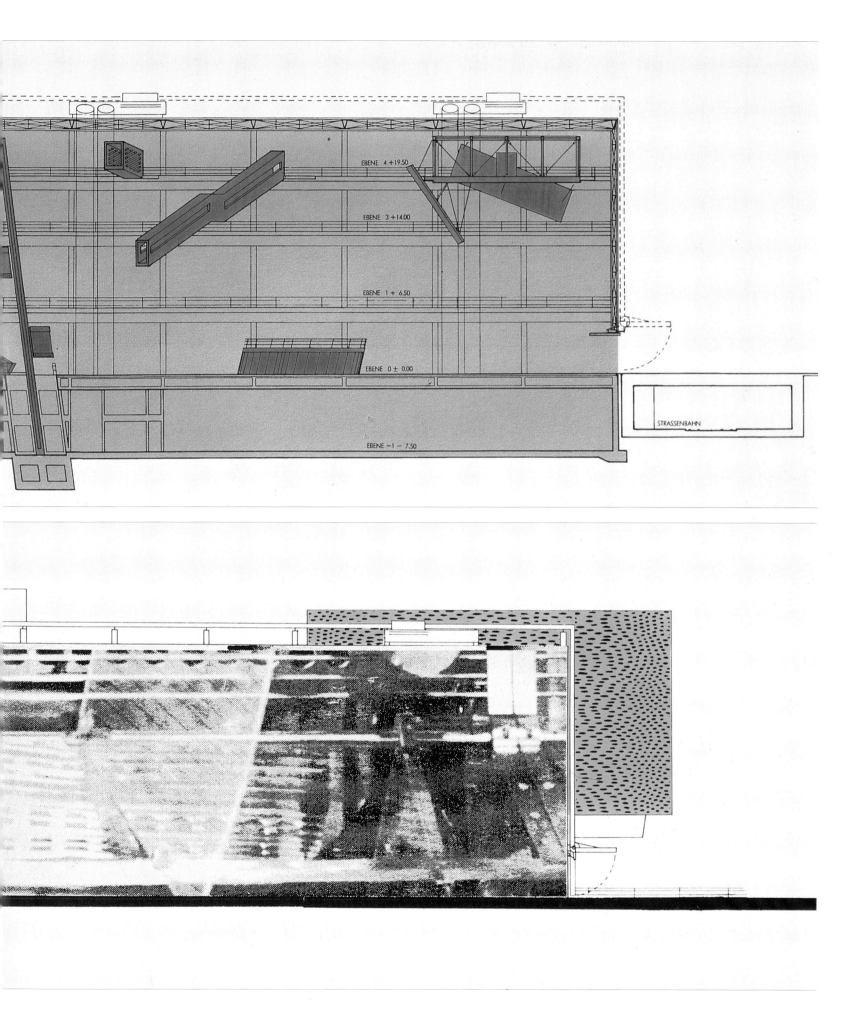

EBENE 4 +19.50

EBENE 3 +14.00

EBENE 1 + 6.50

EBENE 0 ± 0.00

STRASSENBAHN

EBENE ~1 ~ 7.50

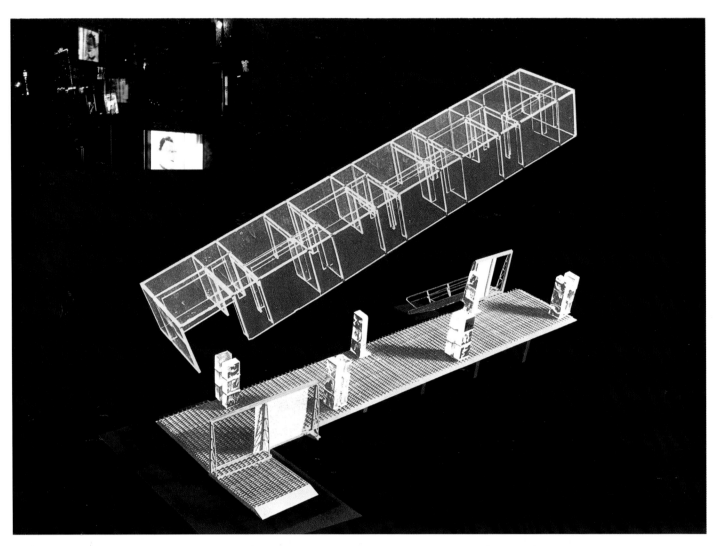

GLASS VIDEO GALLERY, GRONINGEN

The appearance of permanence (ie buildings are solid; they are made of steel, concrete, bricks, etc) is increasingly challenged by the immaterial representation of abstract systems (television and electronic images). The invitation extended by the city of Groningen to design a special environment for viewing pop music video clips was an opportunity to challenge preconceived ideas about television viewing and about privacy. Was the video gallery to be a static and enclosed dark box like the architectural 'type' created for cinema; an extended living room with exterior advertising billboards and neon light; or, rather, a new 'type' that brought what was previously a living room, bar and lounge event into the street in a reversal of expectations?

We proposed THE GLASS VIDEO GALLERY: a 3.6m x 2.6m tilted, inclining, transparent, glass structure. The gallery contains a series of interlocking spaces defined only by a labyrinth of structural 'glass fins' and by the points of metal clip connections. Isolated in this labyrinth are six banks of video monitors used for displaying video clips.

Placed inside one tree-lined roundabout in the city, the gallery is to be seen as an extension of the street condition; except that in these streets borders become indiscernible, monitors provide unstable facades, glass reflections create mirages and limitless space is suggested. The gallery and urban space also have the distinct duality of containing both video objects on display and objects for displaying. They encompass monitor walls viewed through TV dealership store-fronts on the street, along with exhibiting events like those in plastic sex-clip galleries of urban red-light districts.

In this new Video Plaza, one watches and is watched simultaneously.

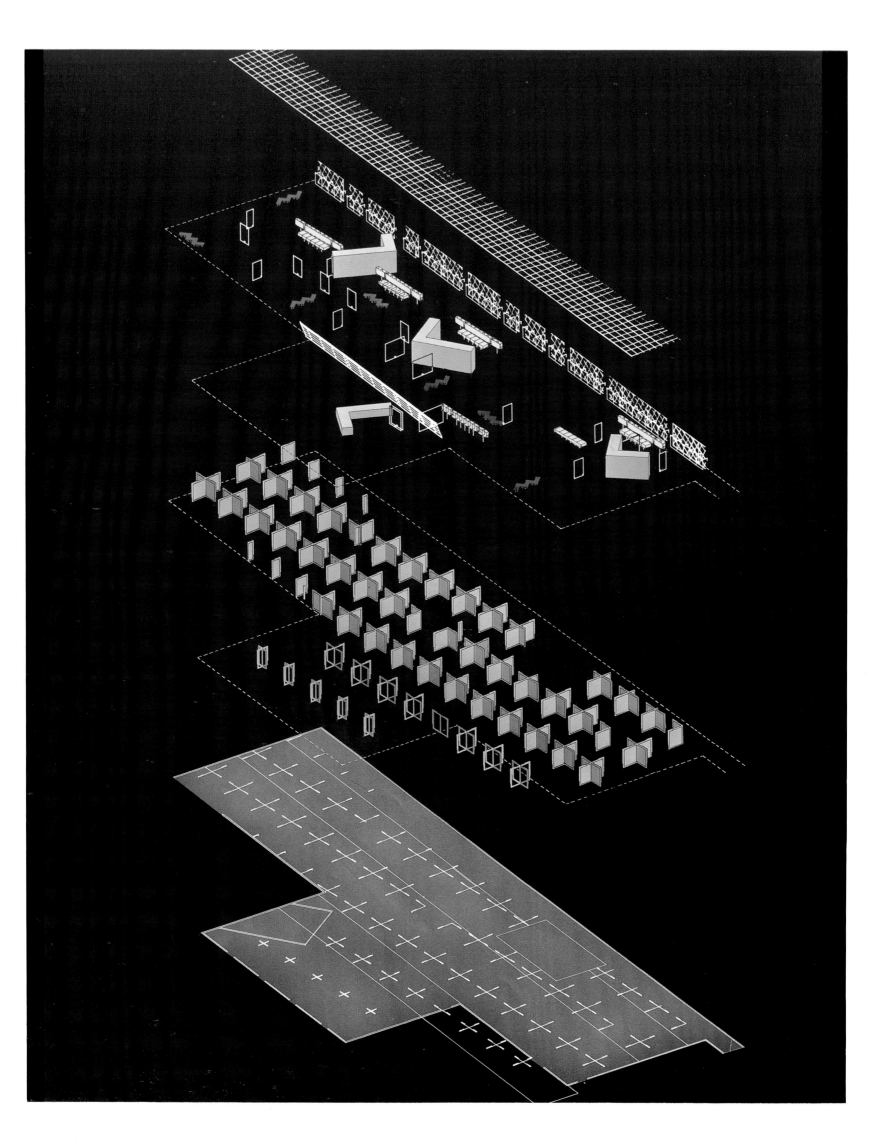

'ART ET PUBLICITÉ' INSTALLATION AT THE CENTRE POMPIDOU
Bernard Tschumi and Jean-François Erhel

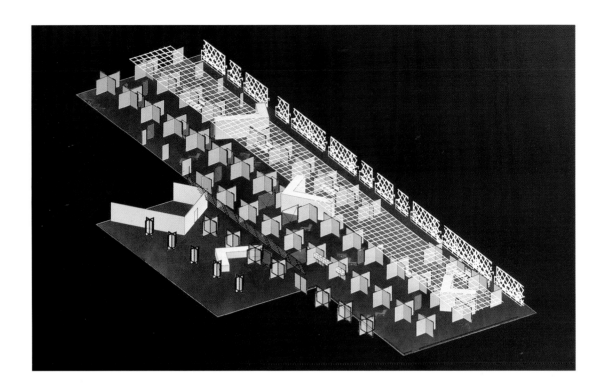

For its 35,000 square-foot fifth floor, the Pompidou Centre wanted an original installation that could accommodate a major exhibition on Art and Advertising ('Art et Publicité'), covering developments extending over the last 100 years, from Toulouse-Lautrec to Barbara Kruger to Volkswagen video clips.

The combination of extremely heterogeneous materials including, on one hand, fragile works on paper and, on the other, raucous life-sized neon signs, suggested two separate parts to the exhibition, the one dedicated to Art and the other to Advertising. However, we decided against establishing an a priori architectural distinction that would arbitrarily define two respective roles. We also felt that these roles were not interchangeable.

Hence we saw our installation as a form of architectural mediation between Art and Advertising. Our concept for the exhibition had more to do with plans of cities and with urbanism than with the layout of interior spaces. Our aim was to develop an autonomous system, which would be independent of both the Pompidou Centre structure and the programmatic content of the exhibition.

We also wanted to reveal, once again, the grand open space of the original Beaubourg plan, removing from it the enclosed 'rooms' and obstructions that had been built by curators over successive years. Thus, our project plays on the idea of endless 'fluid' space and on transparency: it is, indeed, rare to have the opportunity to articulate interior spaces over 100 metres long. The exhibition concept consists of a cross-like grid, marked by 60 intersecting partitions, each 2.80 metres high (the Beaubourg ceiling height averages 4.5 metres.) In plan, these partitions read as a series of crosses, each marking the angle of the spaces they simultaneously define and activate.

Visitors' movement through the exhibition takes place freely among the partition crosses. Semi-transparent fabric panels allow some spaces to be closed while there exists a high degree of transparency throughout the whole 35,000 square feet of the Pompidou Centre. Several 'sight and sound islands' and half-scale reconstitutions of Pavilions by Bayer and Depero, as well as a 'street' along the length of the building, fitted with neon signs and product advertising, present an exploration of elements located at the margins of 20th-century art production.

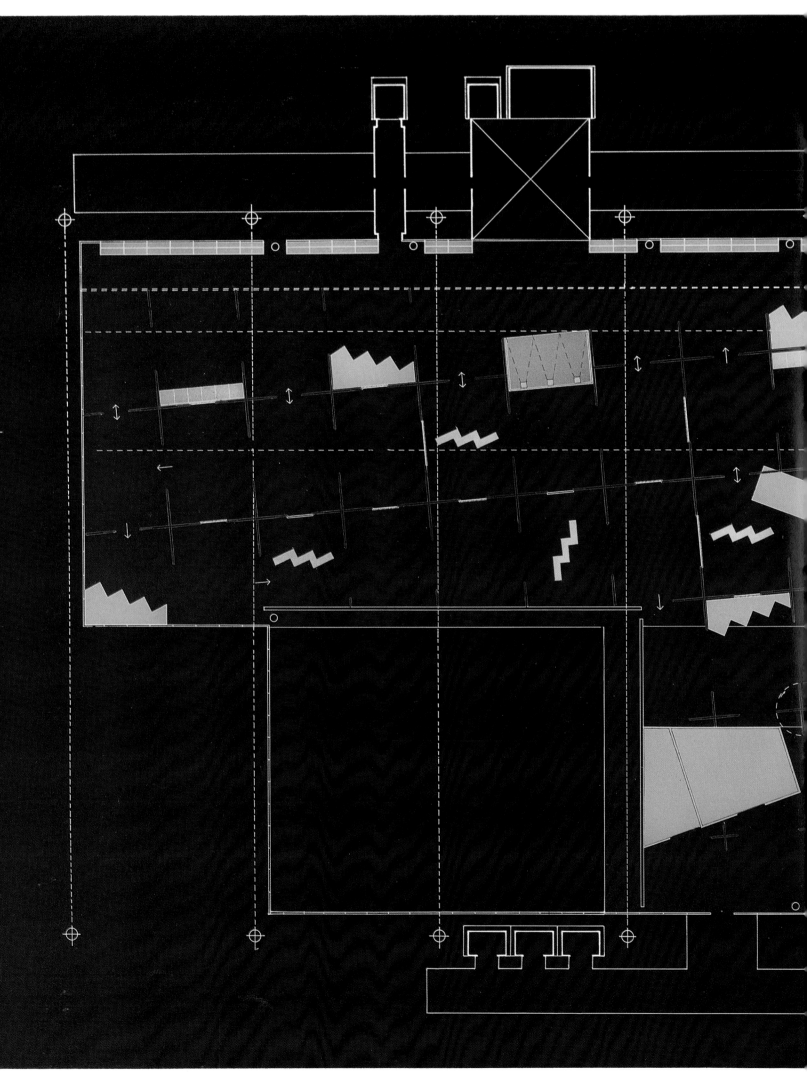

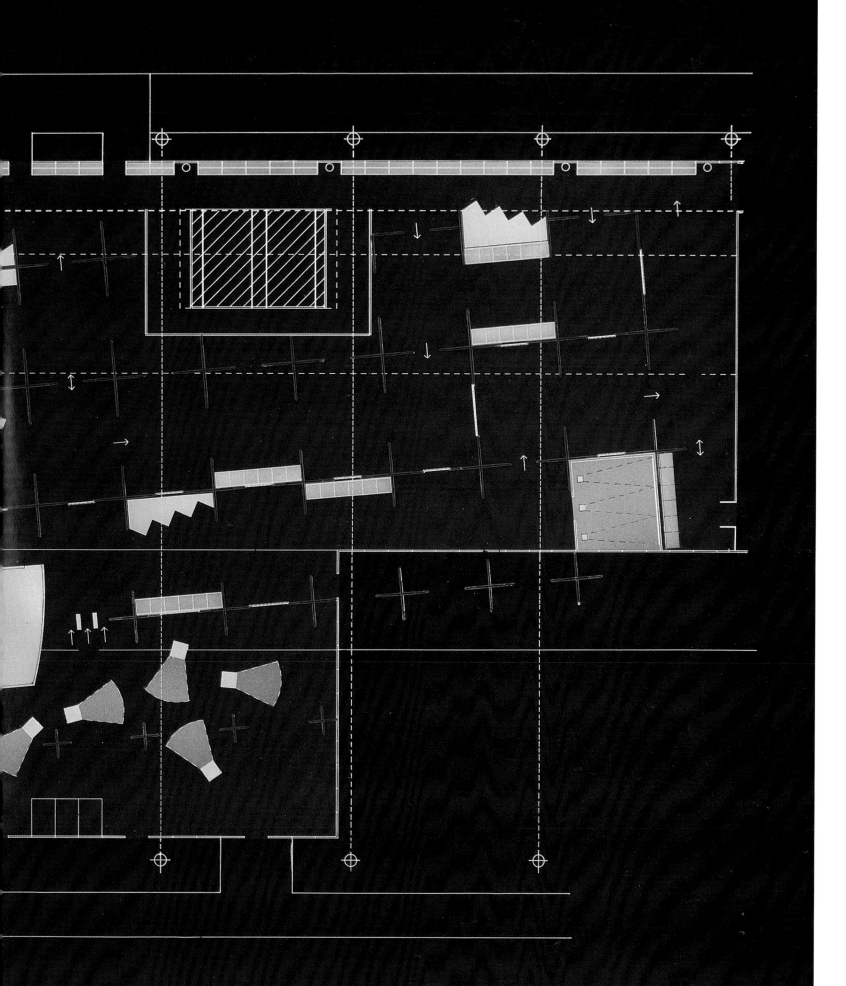

Graduate Work Columbia University

Bernard Tschumi

Student work at Columbia University's Graduate School of Architecture, Planning and Preservation, has taken a definitive new turn, thanks largely to the influence of Dean Bernard Tschumi. The work converges towards a new modern direction, combining an exploration of theory and practice. Tschumi has brought together a number of Studio Critics who, however wide-ranging in either background or ideology, have contributed towards the formation of a body of work that is lucid and has a highly theoretical character, as shown here in a selection of projects from the last three years.

The Advanced Studios in Architecture programmes constitute the final three semesters of study in the school prior to graduation. In the Advanced Studios, a variety of themes are offered by individual critics. These themes carry educational objectives with opportunities for the critics to develop specific areas of work with their students. The Advanced Studios are open to M Arch students as well as to second-professional degree students (MS in Architecture and Urban Design, MS in Architecture and Building Design).

Building upon the basic skills gained in the Core Studios, the Studios aim at developing the students' capacities for investigative thinking and formulating problems rather than mere problem solving. At the end of the 20th century, when the complexity of issues facing urban society is such that politicians, clients and community boards are increasingly ill-at-ease in defining priorities for making our cities and their architecture, it is fundamental for young architects to be able to develop intellectual independence and objectivity.

It is our contention that faced with an ever-changing economic situation, architects will have to define the nature of their profession and that, in the ensuing years, ready-made notions about the traditional role of the architect may have to be reformulated. Among the areas most likely to expand in the near future are those dealing with programmes (what are the new programmes for the 21st century?) and with technology (glue and micro-chips may affect architecture as much as steel construction and elevators once did). Hence, Advanced Studios are constructed in such a way as to challenge students' ideas while promoting a variety of themes that can be explored and developed in a responsible and skillful manner.

The three semesters are characterised by a progression from studios sharing comparable programmatic requirements to final studios with an emphasis on individual statements.

During the first semester of the Advanced Studios (fourth semester, spring, for M Arch students; first semester, summer for MS Building Design and MS Urban Design students), a student is expected to find imaginative and realistic solutions to a specific programme proposed by the individual studio critic. This programme normally entails a choice of medium-sized public buildings in the city and common presentation requirements for all students in the semester.

The following semester (fall, penultimate semester before graduation), a form of specialisation takes place. Instructors are encouraged to propose themes or programmes with distinct emphasis in a particular area of architectural knowledge. These programmes may coincide with the research of the individual faculty member. Hence, programmes are offered with a focus on urban design, on historic preservation, on particular cultures or climates, on low-cost housing, etc.

The final semester (spring) provides students with a unique opportunity to make clear statements about their own attitudes towards the world they are about to enter, building upon the independence afforded by the University context. Within the general or specific theme of investigation proposed by the studio critic, the student is expected to design a key piece of work that addresses relevant architectural and urban issues. Students are encouraged to accompany their design with a written text placing their work in an historical or theoretical context, and with a technical submission outlining the manner in which the proposition can be built.

Steven Holl
studio critic

Tower/House/Observatory
(Volume)

Tomasz Kowalski M Arch

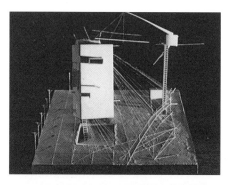

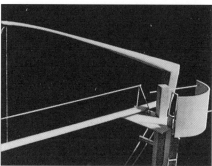

It is precisely the realm of ideas – not of forms or of styles – that presents the most promising legacy of 20th-century architecture. The 20th century propels architecture into a world where meanings cannot be completely supplied by historical languages. Modern life brings with it the problem of the meaning of the larger whole. An increase in the physical size and programmatic complexity of buildings amplifies the innate tendency of architecture towards abstraction. The tall office building, the urban apartment house and the hybrids of commercial complexes call for larger, more open ideas to organise an architectural work. Strategies have developed to return architecture to a level of thought. Organisation of overall form depends on a central concept around which other elements remain subordinate. A concept unites whereas application of an historic style fragments. When a clear idea is the heart of architectural expression, it can be individually related to the circumstance while remaining distinct from a general theory or style.

Zaha Hadid
studio critic

Factory, New York

Veronique Dumont MSBD

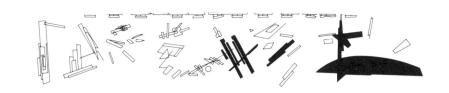

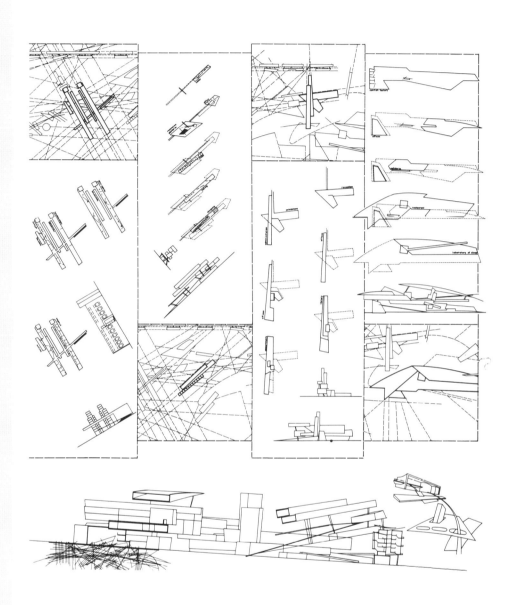

**Hani Rashid and
Mehrdad Hadighi**
studio critics

Monastic Algebra in the
City of Variables
New York, New York

Ahmad Zainulabidin M Arch
Phillip Tefft M Arch
Meiling Leung M Arch
Victor Colom M Arch

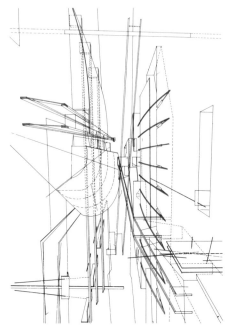

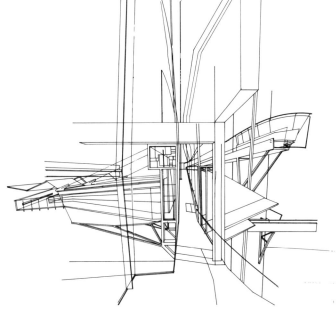

Steven Holl
studio critic

Music School
Palisades Park
New Jersey

Diana Kellogg M Arch

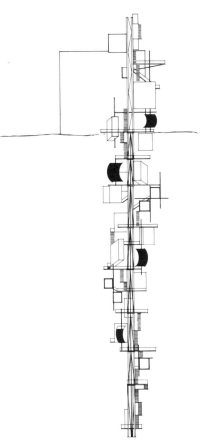

Paola Iacucci
studio critic

Music School
Palisades Park
New Jersey

Eric Anderson M Arch

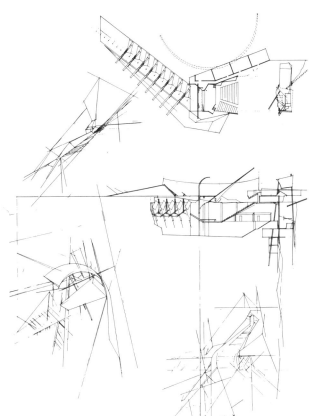

Thomas Hanrahan
studio critic

Tower/House/Observatory

Michael Kennedy M Arch
Eric Robinson M Arch

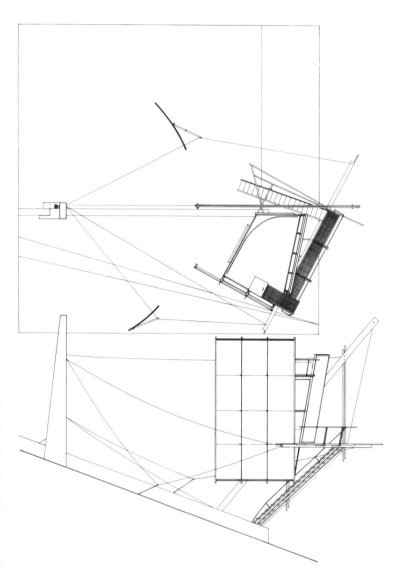

The literal desert is considered as a place for thinking and acting. The desert is a single line, in equilibrium with the body, a boundary between earth and sky. The next line that is made is a disturbance, upsetting the equilibrium, demanding of thought. It is the first desire for an architectural reality. The last line that is made is all that is necessary for this reality, no more or less. Inspired by word, drawn by hand, made real by material, these lines in the desert are the manifestation of thought into a place of action and experience.

Stephen Holl
critic

Vertical Terminal,
Manhattan approach
to Williamsburg Bridge
New York

Jun-Saung Kim M Arch

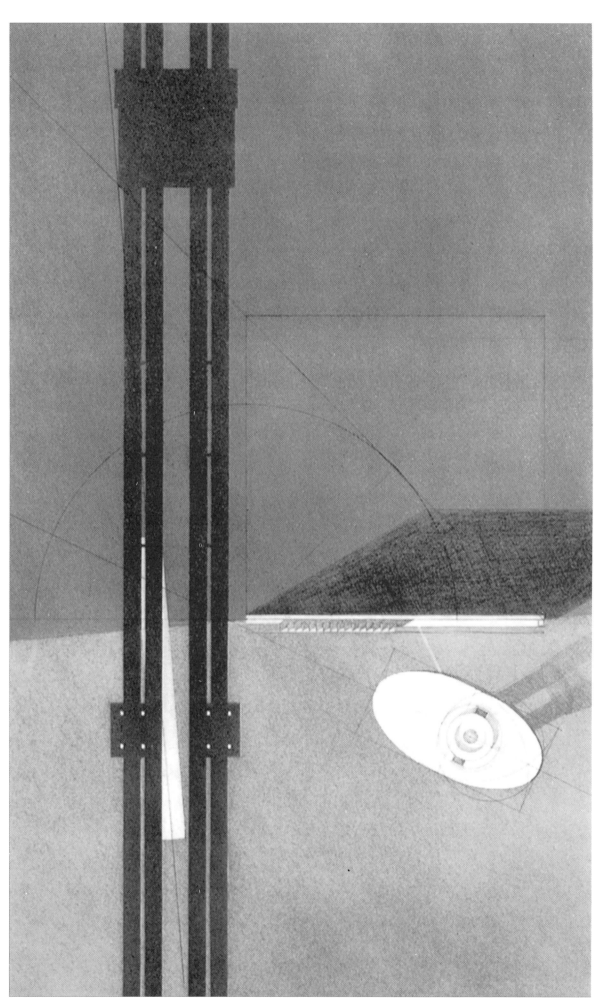

James Tice
critic

An Environmental Teaching-
Conference Center for Alley
Pond, New York, New York

Joseph Sabel M Arch

The intent of this programme is to study a small-scale public building. The educational aim of the term is to develop further synthetic thinking as each student clarifies a concept, finds space and form to meet human activity and realises an idea in material structure. In reality, the studio was pervaded with pressing questions of a broader scope, concerning the institution; architectural thinking as a paradigm for other fields of thought; and design in the face of intellectual and political change. The focus in James Tice's studio of sensitive intervention in the landscape explored public knowledge and responsibility for the environment.
— **Amy Anderson, studio co-ordinator.**

Robert McAnulty
critic

Bridge project

Peter Himmelstein M Arch

3

A bridge is to be designed to span 60 ft across a street between two midtown Manhattan buildings. It must allow pedestrians to cross and must also contain either an observatory, bar, lap pool or aquarium. The programme may be located indoors or outdoors.

Hani Rashid
studio critic

Frontier Incidents

Gro Bnesmo MSBD
Alfonso Perez-Mendez
MSBD

The studio ventured into an uncharted city, an indistinguishable 'zone' on the 'frontier.' Orpheus chanced this place to regain Eurydice; passing through a sea of mercury he came upon it. The ancient Egyptians conceived of a 'House for the Soul,' where the buried Pharaohs were provided with 'houses' in which their souls could dwell in a state of limbo (awaiting the arduous journey into the afterlife). Each culture and millennium has imparted myths and parables about such a place. Angels and Acrobats find their sanctuary here. 'Whichever way you turned, you seemed to be breathing water, to be drinking the air.'

'A poet always has too many words in his vocabulary, a painter too many colours on his palette, a musician too many notes on his clavier.' – Jean Cocteau, 1960.

Kenneth Kaplan
studio critic

Planetary Court
of Arbitration, Moon

Jonathan Pascarosa MSBD

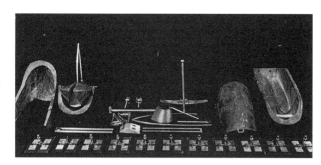

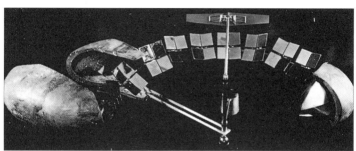

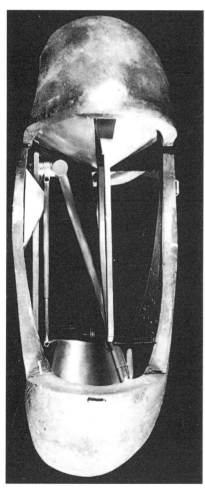

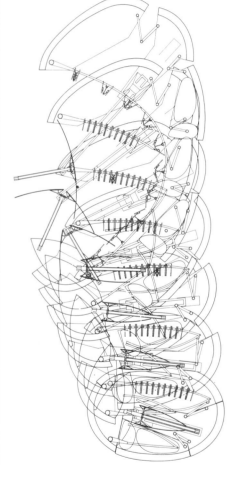

Site: south wall of Rozhdestvensky Crater, South Pole, Moon. The south pole offers the advantage of dark crater bottoms enabling easier heat rejection, while the regions on top remain in constant sunlight, a continuous source of solar power.

 The studio examines the proposal and design of a Court of Planetary Arbitration to be sited on the Moon, the logical location, both geopolitically and economically to establish an initial means to the conflict resolution of international disputes. Based on the model of the International Court of Justice, the judicial organ of the United Nations, this organisation will consist of 15 judges, each of a different nationality, and appointed by the Security Council. Their term of residence will be for nine years. The court, its staff and family members will reside as an integral part of a lunar base which will provide activities of food and material processing, and energy sources for its power plant.

Jeffrey Kipnis
studio critic

Angel Theater

Jennifer Briley MSBD
Meta Brunzema M Arch
Harztan Zeitlan MSBD

The studio will be directed towards a design study of the architecture of performance (theatre, ritual, etc) in an urban context. Particular attention will be given to the questions concerning the relationship between design method and the concretisation of meaning. Context, tectonic viability and project plausibility are requisite considerations.

In order to: a) investigate the engenderment of meaning in plastic processes, b) develop a conceptual vocabulary for that investigation and c) explore design-process consequences of that investigation, the studio will operate throughout under the aegis of a consideration of 'angels.'

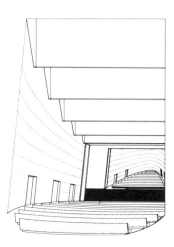

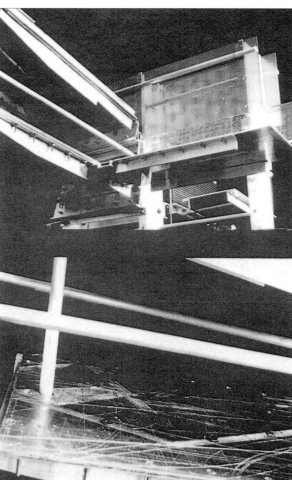

Hani Rashid
studio critic

Simultaneous Cities

Mary Fernando M Arch

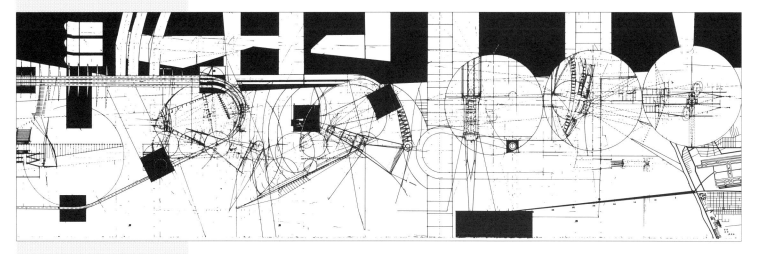

Friction free rail, depart Los Angeles 0800 hr, arrive Tokyo 1100 hr.

Item 1: Formulation and programming of simultaneous structures in Los Angeles and Tokyo that serve as thresholds to both cities vis-à-vis the proposed 'Mag Lev' transportation tunnel beneath the Pacific Ocean. An investigation of the invisible realm that exists between the two cities.

Item 2: Advancements in transportation, telecommunications and the like are certainly in abundance as the century draws to a close. Yet architecture seems little affected by the onslaught of 'progress.'

Item 3: Tokyo and Los Angeles are two cities emerging as centres of extreme import as we move beyond the 20th century. Although they are by no means the only two, they do epitomize much of the dichotomies and disparities of the contemporary urban condition. Providing such a service between these two places certainly can be viewed as a perversity of a world caught up in the 'instantaneous' and the conquest of desire.

Item 4: the self has always been set against an abstraction of the cosmos and that has emerged from reflection on the mapping of our tangible world. Here then is yet a further reduction of time and space as the experiential is all but eliminated.

Items 5-15: The Astrolab and its derivatives;
Surveyor's cross;
Theodolite and Transit;
Leveling and miscellaneous Problems;
Absurd Walls;
The Thick Lens;
Thin Films and Plane Parallel Surfaces;
Barrel Distortion;
Strip division of a wave front;
Zonal Aberration;
An interplanetary 'Flu Machine.'

Leonardo Zylberberg
studio critic

Center for East-West
Exchange, Berlin

Chris Sharples M Arch

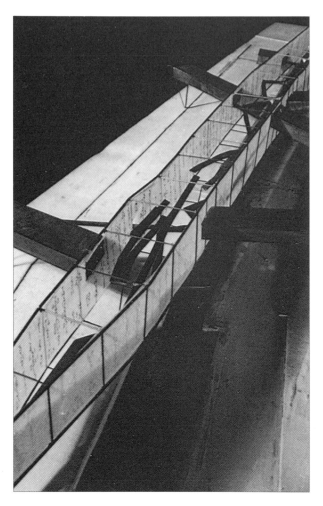

The fall of the wall has abruptly dislocated the physical and cognitive boundaries of one divided Berlin. The former no-man's land and rabbit warren at the edge of two cities has suddenly become an interstitial space of singular importance. Will this zone become a connective tissue to unite the city or a scar that refuses to heal? A generation after the splitting up of Europe, does one struggle to remember or struggle to forget? The proposed programme for the studio was an East-West Exchange Center at the European level, to be located at the wall, between Potsdammer Platz and the Brandenburg Gate.

William MacDonald
studio critic

Photography Gallery and
Loft Studio/Apartments
New York, New York

Minsuk Cho M Arch

The students were asked to explore the architectural implications of the following: 'The guiding law of the great variations in painting is one of disturbing simplicity. First *things* are painted; then *sensations*; finally *ideas*. This means that in the beginning the artist's attention was fixed on *external reality*; then on the *subjective*; finally on the *intra-subjective*.' – José Ortega y Gasset, *Dehumanisation of Art*.

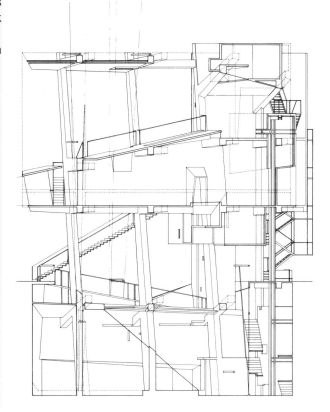

Robert McAnulty
studio critic

Factory for Prosthetic
Devices

Gene Young MSBD

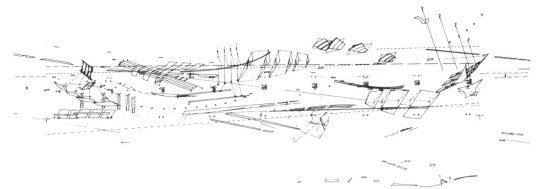

Body Troubles

What are the consequences for architecture of the 'death of Man,' the revered subject of humanism? More importantly perhaps for architecture, what became of his body? All around us, everywhere we turn, the mechanisms of criticism are abuzz with talk of 'the post-structuralist body,' 'body invaders,' 'bodybuildings,' and so on. Clearly the issue of re-writing the classical body is a hot topic these days. An important topic for an architectural discourse whose very foundations we have been taught to believe, rest on its relation to the human figure. Once 'man' has gone, and presumably taken his body along with him, what are we architects left with? Whom do we serve? Where do we look for our formal models? Must we abandon ourselves to the 'precession of simulacra,' revelling in an apocalyptic fin-de-millenium free fall? Must we resuscitate our fallen man phenomenologically or psychoanalytically so as to re-ground our 'destabilised' foundations? Or can we begin to imagine other ways of traversing the horns of this dilemma, routes which map the site of the body and multiply the possibilities for architectural action?

Steven Holl
Paola Iacucci
studio critics

Vertical Terminal
Manhattan
in Year-End Exhibit

Jun-Saung Kim

Mary McLeod
director

Utopia/Heterotopia
Catherine Ingraham

This course examined the possible 'other spaces' of architecture and the city. These other spaces, as Foucault remarks, are both spaces of illusion that reveal how all of real space is . . . illusory' and real spaces, 'as meticulous and well-arranged as ours is disordered, ill-conceived and in a sketchy state.' The utopic condition, ideally a heterotopic condition, is the design of the 'somewhere else' as an *act of critique* of the 'here,' the 'somewhere,' the site and the city. Disneyland, for example, operates (according to Louis Marin and Jean Baudrillard) as a degenerate utopia because it reiterates, rather than critiques, the pathologies of the American city. We analysed three architectural/urbanistic projects: La Villette in Paris, Disneyland (or Disneyworld), and Venturi's re-mapped Las Vegas, in order to discover their utopic/heterotopic power.

History and Theory of the Avant-Garde in Architecture
Joan Ockman

The course took as a primary text Manfredo Tafuri's *The Sphere and the Labyrinth: Avant-Gardes and Architecture from Piranesi to the 1970's*. The history of the avant-garde in architecture was studied in relation to the ideologies of modernism through a chapter-by-chapter reading of Tafuri's account of the confrontation between utopian aesthetics, emergent European and American sociopolitical structures and the modern metropolis. At the same time, the theory and method of 'critical history' was examined as an instrument of architectural criticism in relation to its own subject and other theories.

Deconstructing Meaning in Architecture
Jeffrey Kipnis

25 years after its initial articulations and despite heroic efforts to quiet it, deconstruction continues to insinuate its destabilizing effects into virtually every discipline founded on a tradition of meaning, whether philosophy, history, criticism, psychoanalysis, or law. Yet, for reasons that perhaps emerged as a theme in this seminar, not only is architecture – a late but enthusiastic consumer of deconstruction – uncertain about what to do with it, so it might be noted that deconstruction is as yet equally ill at ease with what to do with architecture. The seminar sought to trace the particularly difficult relationships to be forged among meaning, deconstruction, architectural theory, history and design.

American Architecture: From the Centennial to the Bicentennial
Robert A.M. Stern

A survey of American architecture from the centennial to the bicentennial. Individual lectures are structured along broad thematic lines and supplemented with readings from a wide variety of primary and secondary sources.

Studies in Tectonic Culture
Kenneth Frampton

This course sought to examine the emergence of the tectonic idea in the evolution of modern architecture. As such, it attempted a re-examination of 20th century architecture from the point of view of the role played by structure and construction in the development of modern form. The lecture sequence addressed itself to the so-called autonomy of architecture not so much in terms of space and form but rather from a standpoint of a poetics of construction as this has made itself manifest over the past 150 years.

WOLF PRIX, COOP HIMMELBLAU
ON THE EDGE

The most apt question of our time is: how can we think, plan and build in a world that becomes more fucked up every day? Should we be afraid of these problems and suppress them? As we, Coop Himmelblau, are Viennese, we have a close connection to Freud who taught us that suppression requires a tremendous amount of energy. We would like to spend this energy on projects.

The safe and sound world of architecture no longer exists. It will never exist again. Open Architecture means consciousness and an open mind. In fact, architectural history through the 20th century and into the 90s can be interpreted as a path from a closed to an open space. Ideally, we would like to build structures without objectives in order to release them for free use. As a result, there are no enclosed spaces in our buildings; they just interlace and open up. Complexity is our goal. Architecture, as it was proposed in the 19th century, is over. We have to go for a complexity that mirrors the diversity of world society. Interlaced and open buildings have no divisions: they challenge the user to take over space.

Many people say, 'Oh, your architecture is so aggressive. Why do you slant the pieces? Why do you break it? Why do you twist it?' The simplest explanation is: if you slant a piece of architecture, then you break the function so that very interesting spatial effects can be created.

At the beginning of every lecture, I make a point of showing a slide of our team. This is because team co-operation is one of the most important factors in the work of Coop Himmelblau. My friend and partner, Helmut Swiczinsky, and I have worked closely together on all the projects.

In 1975, we started to try to express our ideas on what we call Open Structures – a reference to Karl Popper's book *Open Society* – by designing loft buildings. At the time, everyone was drawing beautiful little houses with columns, gables and tympanums. This wrong aesthetic angered us so we started to pierce and penetrate buildings with arrows.

Our project for a school in Stuttgart, Germany, was our first attempt at twisting part of a building. This particular scheme created an unusual interwound, interlacing space and although it was never built, we are still very eager to create space for kids.

The Blazing Wing was a happening that we did in 1980. We set alight a courtyard in the middle of a city. As you can imagine, we had to get a lot of permits to do it. In fact, no one at this time knew how to set fire to a 15-metre-high, steel, constructed wing. Although we protected the walls with a water curtain, 21 windows broke because the fire was so hot.

In our 1982 project for a 50-flat apartment complex in Vienna, one of our main goals was to create an open system – a landscape – and keep it free for the use of the occupants. We proposed to begin by building a shell from which people would be able to choose the flat they wanted. In addition, we suggested that the flats should be built economically so that the largest apartments possible could be constructed; the flats would have been at least 2,000-feet long and five-metres high. We calculated that our construction would cost half as much as a normal social housing project; however, no one in Vienna, at this time, dared to go ahead and build it because it would have proved that building expenses for social housing in Vienna are far too high.

So here is just another example of the way we are working in Vienna!

It is only possible to create interwoven spatial systems by getting rid of circumstantial pressure. In order to get complexity in architecture you have to get rid of several things: first, you have to get rid of architectural, historical laws; second, you have to stop thinking about clients; third, you have stop thinking too much about the money you're making; and, finally, you have to stop thinking about cost.

The German word for design – *Entwurf* – is very precise. It shows that it is a very subcon-

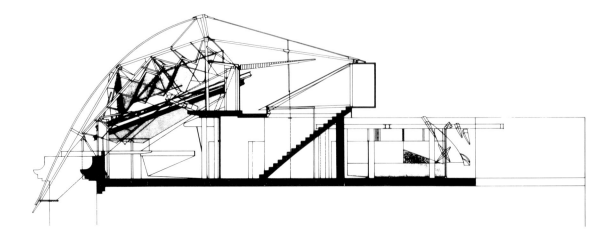

scious and dynamic procedure. In the last couple of years, without knowing where it would lead, we have condensed the moment of conception. We often talk about a project for a long time, without considering the tangible consequences; suddenly, during a drawing, there is a model. This is why team work is so important: while one of us is drawing, the other is converting the drawing into three dimensions by doing the model. If you look at the drawing, it is neither a work-sheet drawing nor a detail, but a multi-faceted ground plan.

This very subconscious procedure allows us to think and to draw very quickly. At the moment of conception we are able to avoid having to think about everything that should be considered afterwards, for example: how can we convince the client? How can we convince the building firm? It makes us very free.

Have you ever seen a leaping whale? I saw one in San Francisco and it was fantastic. I would like to compare this way of drawing with a leaping, champing whale. I was in a boat and the water was very calm but I could feel that there was something moving under the surface. All of a sudden the animal emerged and jumped 15-metres high. You have to imagine it: a 30-tonne, floating, flying object. In our creative procedure, we try to capture this very instance when the animal is moving from water to air. Sometimes we draw with our eyes closed in order to get this moment very quickly down on paper. It does not matter whether we are drawing on the table or on the floor. We are just trying to catch this feeling. You have to be a whale hunter. Success is not guaranteed, but that, too, is Open Architecture.

We have noticed that we complement verbal descriptions with hand and body motions. In art the method is referred to as action painting. It has been popular in Vienna, where there are a lot of artists trying to avoid circumstantial pressure in order to get a feeling – a psychogram of space. For example, during the city planning competition for a city outside of Paris, body language was the first drawing. The energy lines of the head were translated into the model. In between the energy lines, a city was created.

Perhaps a better example is a theatre. There are two concepts: one of the inner shape and one of the outer shape. If you look at a traditional proscenium theatre, the inner concept is the only part of the building visible to the audience. In a competition three years ago, we tried to create a multi-functional stage at Ronacher, from the basement to the roof, so that the whole volume of the theatre could be seen. The major decision for the project was whether we should follow the building codes and do a subterranean programme or ignore the codes and set up a whole new concept for a new theatre.

The site was that of an old theatre so that the brief of the competition veered towards renovation. Since a lot of Viennese architects are rather Po-Mo, we had to decide whether we should diverge from the norm and paint our windows black, or win the competition. So, we won it. We are still filing for this project; however, it is certain that the project will be under construction by next spring.

Body language and architecture – how they play together! One particular object we did in the late 60s contains a space that translates your heartbeat into light and sound. Another of our sculptures translates a facial movement – the expression of the moon – into colour and sound.

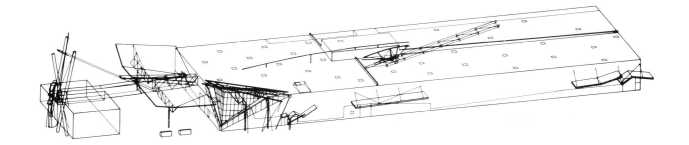

Creating sculptures and environments for museums or galleries was an important part of realising our design procedure. But it did not happen from one day to the next; it only came through practice and through being totally uncompromising. The first project we did in this way was an environment for a German museum. The drawing was done very quickly on March 5th, 1982. When Helmut and I saw the model of it we said, 'Come on, this is so ugly we have to build it!'

The key project for our open design procedure has been the Open House. The house is very complicated and is therefore like the disabled child whom we love very much. We spent a lot of time talking to the client because he was not sure what he really wanted. But this discussion was for defining emotional, rather than functional, needs. The house existed not as a building but as a feeling. The form and the details were not important; what was important was the lighting, the height, the weight and even the view. In order not to be led astray, not even by the graphics, I closed my eyes and used my hands as a graph of the feelings that arose. We did not call it an architectural drawing, but rather a psychogram of the house.

The next step in a project's development from that of drawing and model is the transformation into details and construction. It is in this phase that these seemingly arbitrary forms make sense. For instance, a slanted box allows us to create a double shell construction that can be used as a passive energy system because of its versatile, insulating capacity. The client may be convinced that he wants to use the house as it was intended: he moves into it and inhabits it, then he decides where he wants to sleep, where he wants to live and where he wants to read. The client may or may not choose to do this – that, also, is Open Architecture.

Although it is not immediately important, construction becomes crucial at the second or third step. In order to build this suspended, floating feeling, you have to know about more than columns and beams. In fact, our structural engineer is the only real Deconstructionist in our group; only he knows how to calculate by separating every part and then can put it back together again.

Anyway, this first client of ours was from our home town Vienna. The project, however, was publicised by being printed on the cover of a book. We got a call that resulted in a commission to build the same house in Los Angeles. I am sorry to say this, but we did not win the race against time: our American client was very old and he died before we could start building it. Everything was finished so we bought back all the plans, even the land. Now we are trying to sell the house as a package. In two weeks it will be sold at an auction at Sothebys. I have heard that Kim Basinger is very interested in it.

Our first sketch of the roof-top remodelling in Vienna shows every element and concept that we like to emphasise in a building in the later stages. This project is a kind of corner solution. In Vienna, when people build on corners, they all try to put up little towers, lovely cube-shaped constructions. Needless to say, we did not do this! We decided that our glass, cupola-topped scheme should be a way of playing with closed and open panels. This is the way we normally resolve a corner solution! Another important element is context. For us, context is not a matter of building in proportion to neighbouring structures. Instead, we broke up and crossed over the old roof with a transversal flashlight which came from the

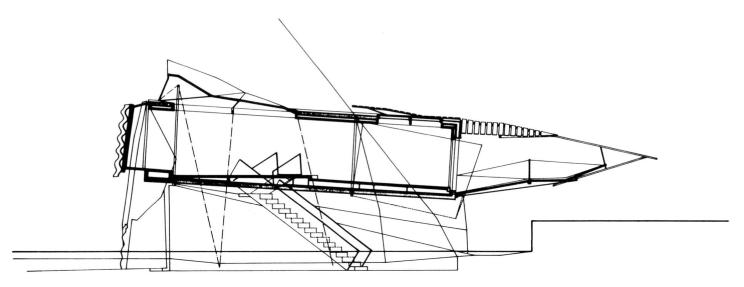

street and effectively created new space. Another prominent aspect of any project is the view, both the inside and the outside view. The inside and the outside have a relationship. You have to know that the area in which we built this conversion is heavily protected as a landmark; therefore, we were not allowed to change anything about the roof-top. So, how did we deal with this? We went to the mayor of Vienna and said, 'Look, we are not only architects, we are artists too. Please look at the model: this is a piece of art. How can the building commission chuck away a piece of art?' And he said, 'You are right.'

Our brief, in this case, was to build an office with a meeting room. We constructed a balcony in order to provide access from the roof garden to the meeting space. As I have already stated, a flash-light came in from the street, crossed the whole project and broke up the old roof. It was not, however, aggressive. We are not destructive; we only destroy in order to create new inside and outside spaces.

When we showed the construction model of the roof-top conversion, at the MoMA show, a lot of American colleagues came to us and told us that they enjoyed the project, but they did not believe it could be built. This really amused us as it was under construction at the time.

There are a great deal of advantages in dealing with a client once a building is under construction. The view of the first sketch of the roof conversion was the strongest from the inside to the outside so that the structural glazing pieces, which make up the cupola, are arched to the outside. The client however complained about this. He asked us to cover it. So we said 'OK, we can cover it and hide it but it will cost money.' So he of course said, 'OK, leave it!'

We love to use the sculptural quality of light in our work. The slit of light created by a light beam penetrating a wall is one of the best examples of this. When the sun shines, an arrow of light illuminates the wall opposite. In the evening, however, the client can become the creator as he makes an artificial light beam from the inside out.

Another strategy, characteristic of our work, is to be very economical on the parts of a building that we have to execute (such as the side wings of an office) in order to save money for the parts that we want to emphasise.

I will give you an example of yet another way we design. We were once commissioned to enlarge a staircase. The owner of the house, however, was not satisfied with what we had drawn up; he said that the staircase must have windows. We did not like having these windows, these light-slits, so we crossed them and built a correction of the first sketch. It took us two years to convince everyone to build it. I still do not believe that the client could imagine what this project would look like, but now he is going around like Alice in Wonderland. He is so proud of it. We were proud of it too when we first saw it built – it was like a diamond glowing on a roof-top.

We do not always design with our eyes closed; sometimes we work the other way around. We built a factory at about the same time that we did the staircase. Our first sketch was a white box, with no details. We both added and cut away some important parts before sticking them back together in a very strange way. It was a very economical structure to build; there is no detailed production hall. We thought we would let a factory do what a factory should do

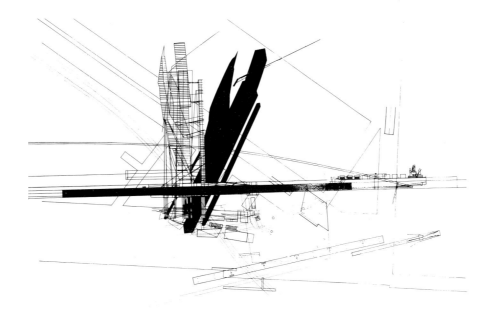

– produce things. As it is not a creative environment, it is a very economic structure.

Indeed, the factory is a white box with little more than three details. Since a freeway passes to the side of it, we called this facade the 100-Mile Power Facade. On the other side, there is a very small street going past it so we decided to design everything on this as on a 30-Mile Power Facade. The facades meet on a glazed corner, at a glass edge, indicating that there is a special room for presentation within. Let's call it a lobby! Overall, however, the factory, from both inside and outside, looks like a multi-functional space – empty.

Our project Dancing Chimneys II was quite different as it posed a builder's question. It made us ask ourselves: why do stacks always stand very straight? We did not, however, build the answer; we really built the question. We call it Dancing Chimneys II because from every angle it looks very different and, in addition, if you run around the energy centre extremely fast you can see the chimneys dancing. But you have to be very fast!

We have a project on our tables, right now, that explains very precisely what we mean by twisted and slanted building parts. Originally, it was a competition – which we won – to design an addition to an existing hotel. The hotel has a huge park and lake, so we agreed to open the park and twist the whole building complex into it. By twisting or slanting just one level of the four-storey high building, we can gain another level that we can use for, let's say, a sauna. The problem is that we cannot set stilts into the lake because you cannot touch nature in Vienna; you have to build around trees instead of through them. Our solution allows us to create a building that cantilevers about 100 feet. It would have been much easier to have stilts, however, if it had been permitted. I have to admit this is just an excuse because cantilevers allow us to define the energy lines, cut off from the air, that create space.

Another scheme that we are presently working on also uses cantilevers. It is for an office building in Vienna. Part of the structure twists in order to incorporate both nature and a recreation area into the building. The cantilevers have two other advantages: first, a lot of money and room can be saved on staircases because there are ramps which go from the basement to the top of the building; second, such a concept is very convincing for the client. Actually, by twisting and slanting things you gain a lot of special spatial situations.

Architecture needs at least three standing points to be stable. In the last two or three years we have been working on the third leg. We really want to get rid of it. In our first trial with this, there were two legs and the third leg was, of course, not a standing leg but more of an attention leg. In the chair that we designed the third leg was a very thin spiral. The first time we almost got rid of it completely was in our 40-foot tower for Osaka Expo. This seemingly third leg does not support anything because it ends in a needle-point. So we replaced the third leg with a very thin tension rod which makes the structure stable.

By getting rid of the third leg, the other two legs are ready to move. It has become very important for us to create moveable things, not only spaces but parts too. For instance, an office project we did is closed, not by a normal door but by a five-metre long and three-metre high glass wall with a sliding door. If it is five-metres long, where do you go?

We have also started to move around small parts in our projects. For instance, we designed a kitchen that has both vertical and horizontal movement in its bar table. It is complex: if you move this bar everything else moves too. It is very disturbing, but it is fun to cook because you are forced to be creative!

Our sports stadium in Vienna has a removable roof as well as a moveable bridge that is a skating area. There is an ice bar as well so that in the summer you can skate from the sporting rink to the bar. The elevator and the bridge also go up and down.

In the Japanese bar that we designed the main parts, too, are moveable. The bar not only moves on the inside but it actually breaks through the exterior roof. You know how these Japanese sites are all the same, very refined, very small. You have to go upward to make a door. There are six bars ascending from the basement and they all have very different slanted floors. You can actually rent the most expensive champagne bar. The more you pay in one of the bars, the higher you are elevated. I am sure there is only one position because everyone wants to be on top.

So, moveable parts are at the forefront of our latest projects. When we talked to our Japanese client for the first time, he was very concerned about Open Architecture. He thought that we did not need to use glass for the roof-top. The Japanese like their bars closed with no windows. So we designed a closed space; the only open space is in the roof where there is an overview of the city.

The way we got this project was very funny. I got a call from Tokyo and was asked, 'Do you want to build a bar in Tokyo?' I said, 'A bar, a restaurant, OK, why not?' So, I met the client. He had a bunch of publications about Himmelblau in his hand and said, 'I want you to make a bar for us and it should look like this, this and this; and this is the building you should build within it.' I looked at this building and said, 'How can we do that to a Post-Modern building? I don't know if the architects would be very pleased if we started penetrating their walls.' And he looked at me and said, 'OK, what do you want to build?' I said, 'We want to build buildings with moveable rooms and flying staircases and burning walls and things like that.' And he said very seriously, 'We will do that.' I said, 'Oh, God, I know, I know.' He then took out his filofax. It was no calendar, but packed with city maps. On every city map there were red pointers. He showed me, 'This is Sydney, this is Toronto, this is New York. This is my property.' And we ended up in Fukuoka where he said, 'Here, you will build.' I said, 'Yeah, why not? Of course.' And snap – a photographer came and there was the contract.

When we came to prepare this project for Fukuoka, I could not go to Tokyo so we made a video in Los Angeles. Consequently, we got a letter and the client said that this project was too good for Fukuoka, he had a better site in Sapporo. He sent me over to look at the site. It was perfect. We are now in the process of moving this project to Sapporo.

We have a second office in Los Angeles where we have had a commission to do a shopping centre. It is a combination of a bar, two restaurants, two bookstores and several boutiques. It is on a corner of Melrose Street. Melrose, in LA, is the only street where people walk rather than drive. So we decided, since it was a very special site, to place the bar on the corner and make the bar out of moveable platforms. It is the same game as the Japanese project: the more you pay, the higher you are. I am curious to see how the three bars will compete – who pays more and so forth. For us it is the first time since the open house project, done in Europe, that we have really had to think how to build in Los Angeles. We are used to the Viennese tradition of having to do detailing thoroughly. In California, we are having to deal with splitting up boxes because building boxes in Los Angeles is a game – the boxes should last five years. We have tried to make the box more complex than it is.

Another project we have is for the Groningen follies. Several of our friends, including Zaha Hadid and Bernard Tschumi, were also invited to participate in this video exhibition. We all had to choose two programmes. We chose the rock 'n' roll and the sex programmes; then, we had to design a folly that would provide the space in which 40 people could watch the videos. We have placed our folly in the river so that it is only accessible by bridge.

I think the last lecture I did here was three years ago at the AA. When I showed my last slide, at the end, I said that I would be back if the project was built. Well, I came back! I will handle my next two projects in the same way. They are an office building for LA and a hotel tower for Vienna. The latter is not just a hotel, it is a hybrid building with an infrastructural programme: the lobby and apartments are on the top with the hotel in between. I promise, if this is built, I will be back to give you another lecture.

COOP HIMMELBLAU
THE 'OPEN HOUSE', MALIBU, CALIFORNIA

Created from an explosive-like sketch drawn with eyes closed. Undistracted concentration. The hand as a seismograph of those feelings created by space. It was not the details which were important at the moment, but the rays of light and shadow, brightness and darkness, height and width, whiteness and vaulting, the view and the air.

The house – slanted body and vaulted skin – is 2,050 sq ft. The entry, a stairway.

The current of energy in the sketch is translated into statics and construction. The building itself – resting on three points and taut – almost floats. The construction of the taut elements makes a double-glazed skin possible.

Protection of the building brings about a double-shelled construction that is suitable for its passive energy concept, as well as ever-possible alteration. There is no predetermined division of the living area. That could or could not result after the completion of the house – that too, is Open Architecture.

This project is planned for completion in 1990, in Malibu, California.

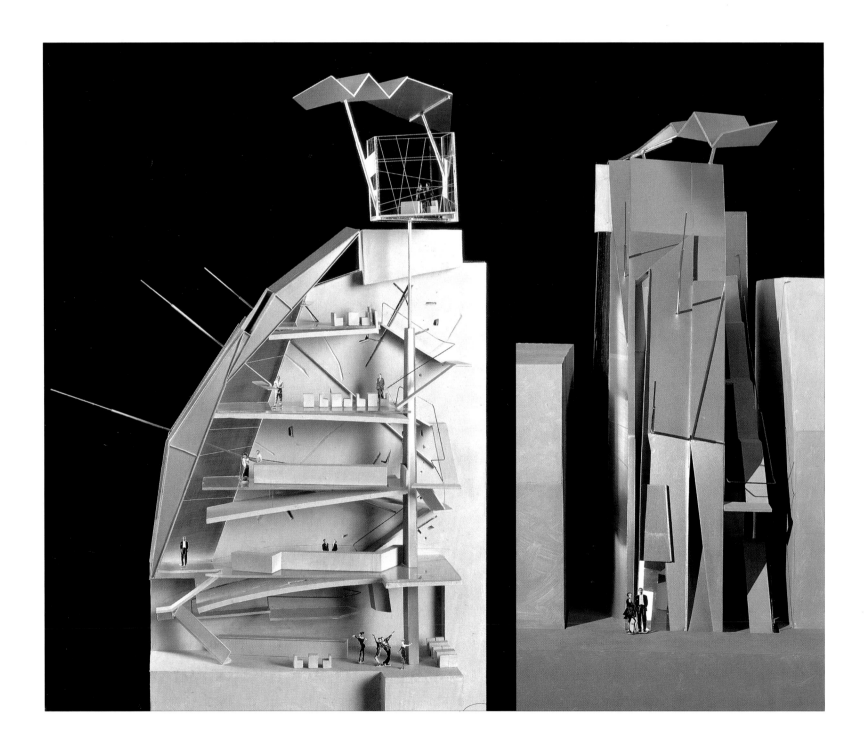

A four-storey restaurant building with five different bars. The Champagne Bar is in a special room which can move up and down through the roof.

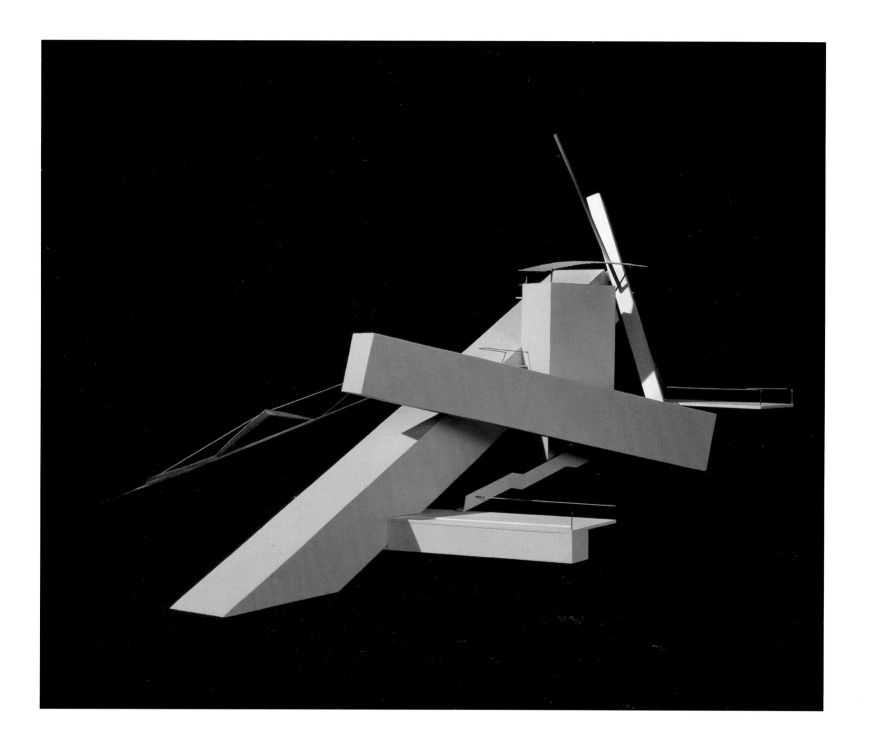

The building site is very inconveniently divided. An isthmus juts through it, creating a
northern plateau and a southern slope. We decided to design the building in accordance with
the precipitous southern slope. The first sketch and the first model depict the concept. Two
arms – we call them the city-view arm and the ocean-view arm – are affixed to the slope in
the shape of an 'x'. Flying platforms, accessible rooftops and a tower all tie the volume
together.

ARQUITECTONICA
RECENT PROJECTS

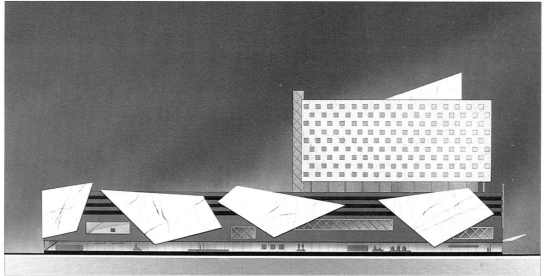

Miracle Center, Miami, Florida

This is a mixed-use complex on an urban site in the Coral Gables area of Miami. The project includes 230,000 square feet of retail shops, ten movie theatres and a health club on three levels. Above the retail, there is parking for 1,000 cars and an 18-storey, 100,000 square-foot tower containing 98 residential apartments.

Shopping Complex, Atlanta, Georgia
This 120,000 square-foot shopping complex is located in a revitalised area of downtown Atlanta. A group of two-storey buildings takes advantage of the sloping site, allowing primary access at both levels to restaurants, cafes, night clubs and speciality stores. The complex focuses on a central plaza and reflecting pool.

Center for Innovative Technology, Fairfax and Loudoun Counties, Virginia
This is a master plan and first phase construction for a 650,000 square-foot office and research complex in suburban Washington DC. Phase I includes the headquarters for the Commonwealth of this Center, the headquarters for the Software Productivity Consortium and a common facility which includes an exhibition hall, auditorium, briefing and press rooms, classrooms, fitness centre and dining facilities. The buildings sit atop a four-storey parking garage with a landscaped roof deck.

OSAKA FOLLIES

The creation of a society of plenty and charm for the 21st century was the theme for the International Garden and Greenery Exposition at Osaka: based on the proposal of Arata Isozaki, one of the Expo's general producers, 13 follies were designed by a dynamic selection of invited architects. The architects were allocated similar budgets and the basic formula for size was a 7.5 metre cube. We present here a selection of the realised projects.

A gateway for expressing the harmony between man and nature, the folly addresses a problem facing almost every urban area whose growth tends to alienate nature, pushing it outside the city limits . . . The structure, precariously balanced by the use of two cables, reminds us that the interface between man and nature is both tenuous and in need of being addressed daily.

Morphosis

Follies, to us, are prospective studies of future buildings; elements of the sculptures can and will appear within our up-coming projects.
The Expo folly in Osaka is therefore only seemingly a 25 metre high tower within an observatory platform. The elements of the tower – the head, body and construction – are, in fact, outlined elements of a six-storey high building made of steel and glass.

Coop Himmelblau

With the 20th century now drawing to a close, this folly, which I transformed into design, is an homage to slope, that flash of lightening which appeared when the curtain was raised at the beginning of this century.

Ryoji Suzuki

BOLLES-WILSON

MORPHOSIS
COOK & HAWLEY

ZAHA HADID
MOONSOON RESTAURANT
Sapporo Japan 1990

The project as an interior contradicts its exterior enclosure. The constraints of the conventional building created the desire to break away. The result is a hybrid of compressed, dynamic inside and static outside. The two-fold programme of a restaurant with formal eating and relaxed lounging is stretched between two synthetic and strange worlds of opposite character: fire and ice.

The ground floor in cool greys (materialised in glass and metal) was inspired by the seasonal ice buildings of Sapporo. The tables emerge as sharp fragments of the raised level from the rear, drifting like ice across the space.

Above the ice chamber whirls a furnace of fire in brilliant reds, yellows and oranges. A bar which tears through the ceiling of the ground floor spirals up to the underside of the dome like a fiery tornado bursting a pressure vessel. Elsewhere a plasma of biomorphic sofas hybridises eating with lounging, allowing for an infinite configuration of seating types with moveable trays and sofa backs that plug in at any point.

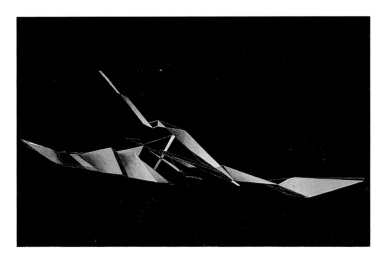

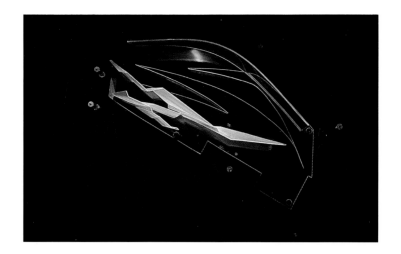

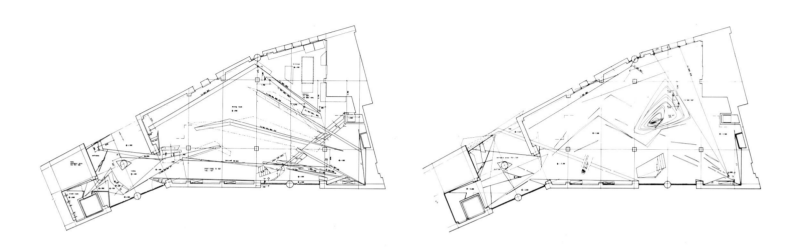

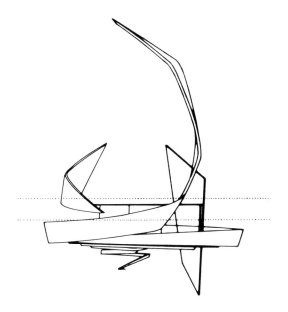

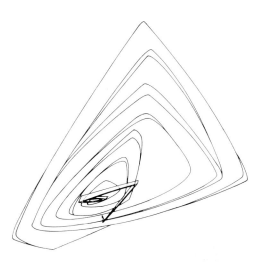

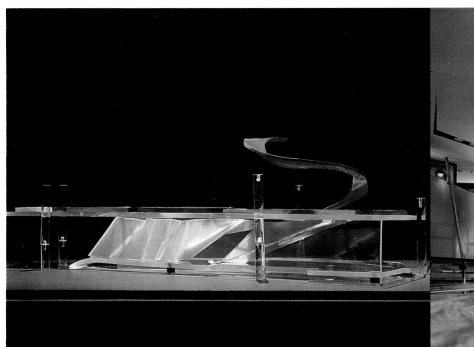

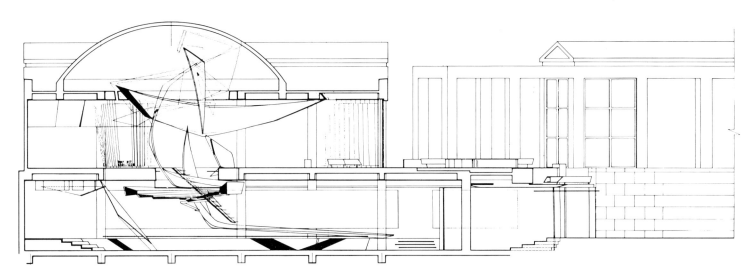

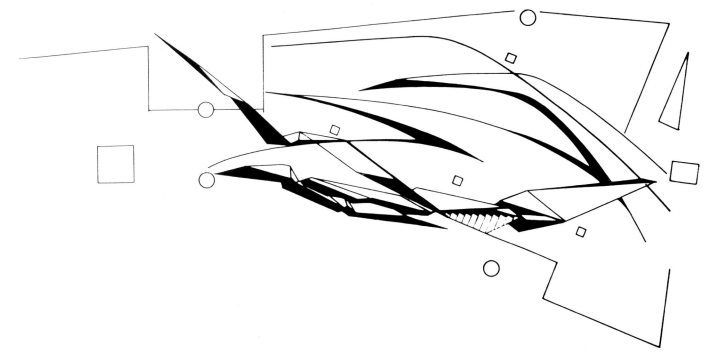

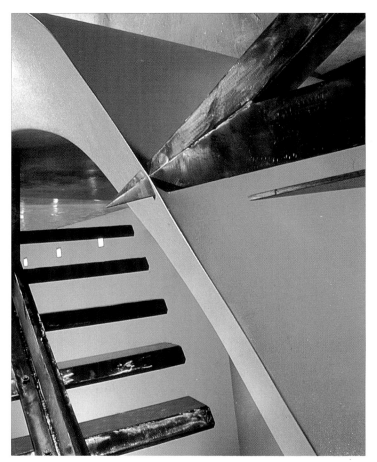

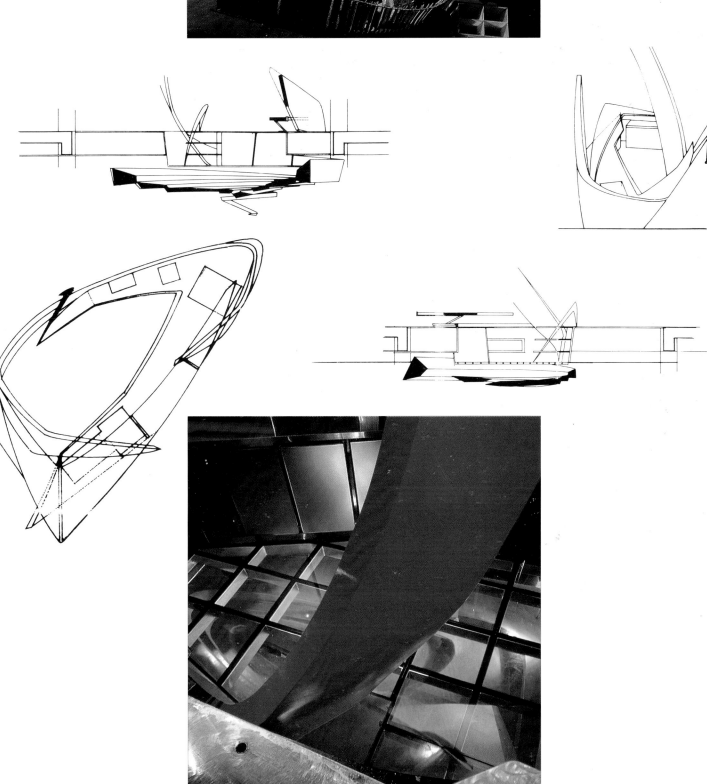

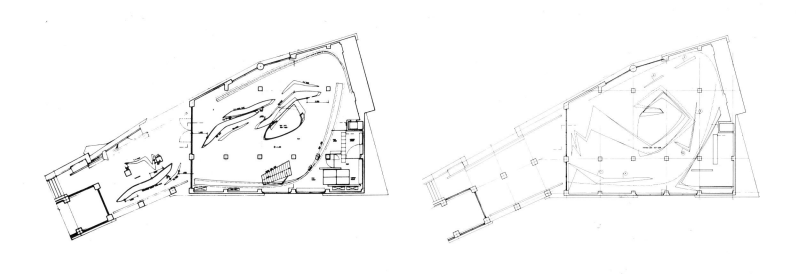

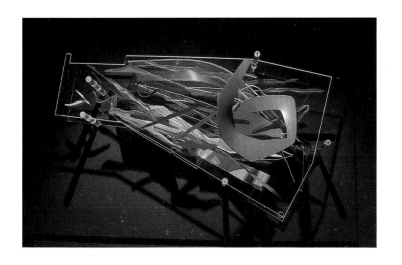

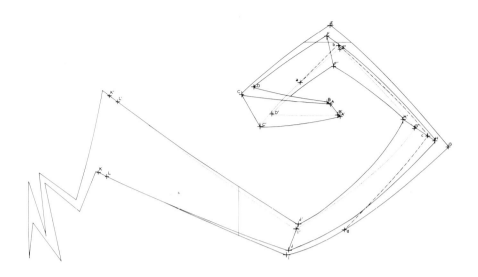

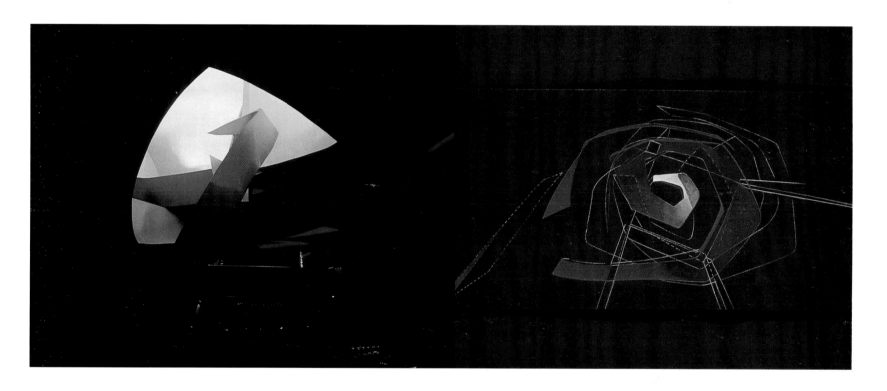

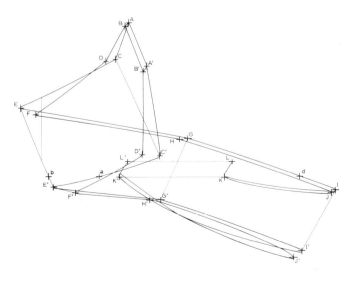

Credit List

Design Team: Zaha Hadid with Bill Goodwin, Shin Egafhira, Ed Gaskin, Edgar Gonzalez, Kar Wha Ho, Brian Langlands, Urit Luden, Yuko Moriyama.

Upstairs seating and objects: Zaha Hadid with Micheal Wolfson.

Models: Dan Chadwick.

Producer: Axe Company Limited.

Quality Control at Tokyo Office of Zaha Hadid: Satoshi Ohashi.

Client: Jazmac.

Photography: Paul Warchol.

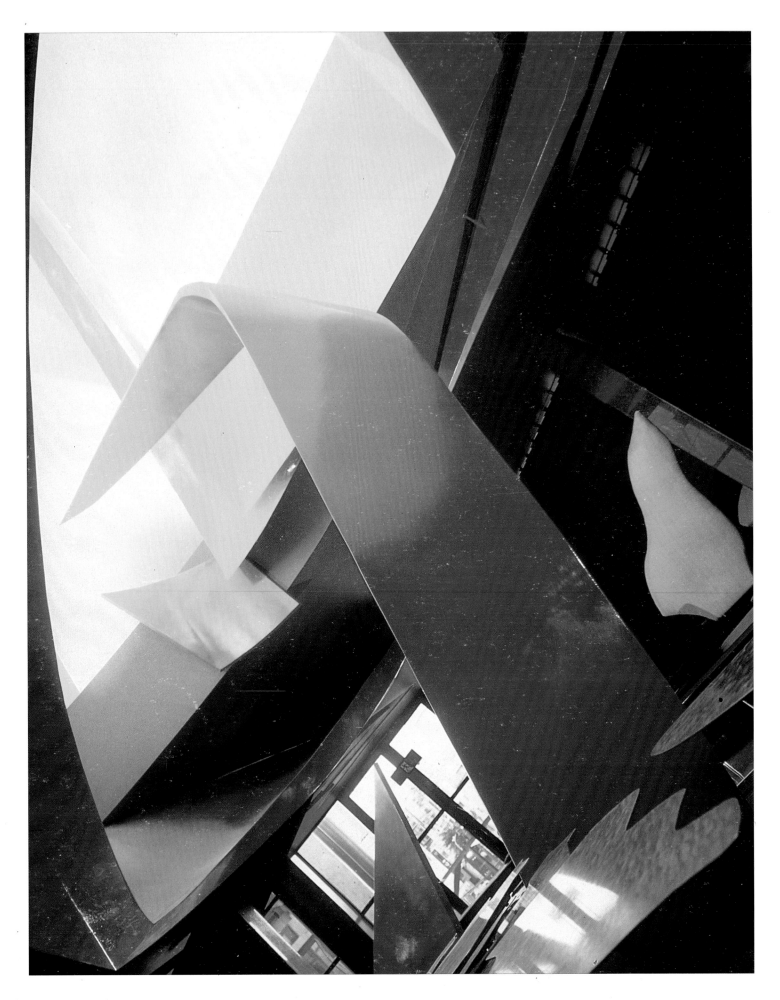